150TH ANNIVERSARY 1833-1983

The Making of
JOHN MENZIES

Leslie Gardiner

Foreword

The Victorians were a remarkable race. They changed a small agricultural island into the first industrial state, greatly benefiting their descendants. My great grandfather epitomised their virtues of honesty, industry, patriotism and ambition. He founded his firm in 1833 and our 150th anniversary seems a suitable occasion to record the story.

Company histories, though of great interest to those who work in companies and to the founding families, are not, on the whole, of general appeal. The author, Leslie Gardiner, is to be congratulated on writing not only a history of the company but also a chronicle of literary life from the 'Golden Age' of Edinburgh to the present day.

The book records the devotion of generations of employees whose efforts to give good service to our customers were a prime factor in the growth of the company. This seems an appropriate place to pay tribute to them, both past and present, and this I gladly do.

John Maxwell Menzies, chairman.

Contents

Chapter 1 'A calling of very high order' page 5

Chapter 2 'Up a few steps' page 13

Chapter 3 'A very striking change' page 25

Chapter 4 'Prompt despatch is the secret' page 35

Chapter 5 'The whole tempo changed' page 43

Chapter 6 'The arrangement is a splendid one' page 49

Chapter 7 'Porridge and the shorter catechism' page 55

Chapter 8 'Open for business as usual' page 61

Chapter 9 'If dry leave paper in doorway' page 71

Chapter 10 'From Thurso to Penzance' page 79

Chapter 11 'A business greatly extended' page 87

The Menzies Dynasty page 93

Some Menzies Directors page 96

Acknowledgements

©John Menzies plc 1983

Printed by
John Bartholomew & Son Ltd
Edinburgh Scotland

Text written by Leslie Gardiner

Book design by Forth Studios Ltd
Edinburgh

Reproduction by Friarsgate Studio
Ltd of Beverley

Typesetting in Garamond Book
by Ace Phototypes Ltd Edinburgh

Paper Royal Sword Matt 135gsm

Book bound by
Hunter & Foulis Ltd Edinburgh

Illustrations

City of Edinburgh Museums and
Galleries:
Creech's bookshop

Edinburgh Museum of Childhood:
Playing cards
Boys of the Empire
Chatterbox

McLean Museum and Art Gallery
Inverclyde District Council
P S Guinevere

W H Smith & Son Ltd:
Railway bookstall

Strathclyde Regional Archives:
Sir Robert Graham

Edinburgh City Libraries:
Slateford Aqueduct
Scotsman 1st Edition
Royal High School
Waterloo Place
Punch
Princes Street
Tait's magazine
Blackwood's magazine
John Sobieski Stuart
Charles Edward Stuart
Murray's diary

Leslie Gardiner:
Stagecoach

1

'A calling of very high order'

'A calling of very high order'

There was uproar at a literary banquet in Edinburgh when the poet Thomas Campbell rose to propose the health of the Emperor Napoleon. (This was early last century, when a toast to Napoleon was about as popular with the British as a toast to Hitler in our own times.) "Do not mistake me, gentlemen," said Campbell. "The Emperor Napoleon is a monster and a tyrant, I agree. He is the enemy of the human race. But let us give credit where credit is due. Let us never forget the Emperor Napoleon once shot a bookseller."

Campbell spoke, of course, for disappointed authors. He had had problems, like Napoleon in his youth, getting money out of his bookseller. And by 'bookseller' he meant 'publisher'. In those days, when the press gang and the militia ballot were in force, when George III still reigned and Walter Scott anonymously issued *Waverley* (7th July 1814) and the city fathers of Edinburgh were tempting people to desert the Old Town and go and live in the New with promise of life-long freedom from rates and taxes . . . in those days the booksellers of Scotland and England frequently made arrangements with authors and printers and actually published many of the books they sold. According to David Wyllie, who opened the first bookshop in Aberdeen, they did more than that:

'New books were delivered from the printer in their naked sheets and the bookseller had to read them and clothe them'

–to correct the proofs, fold the sheets, cut and stitch them into boards, cover them with drab paper and stick a small printed title on them. He would then put the finished articles on his shelves, all looking alike in the sombre battledress of every pre-Victorian publication, and hope that someone would come in to buy them.

Or hope not, as the case might be. Your old-fashioned Scottish bookseller didn't care for too many customers. James Thin, founder of the bookshop in Edinburgh which still bears his name, remembered the bookhawker Johnston who kept a stall on the Earthen Mound, the carriageway between Old Town and New. Seen packing up and turning people away in mid-afternoon, Johnston would explain:

'Ah've sold so many the day, Ah'm feart Ah'll have none left for the morn.'

Robert Brown, a Peninsula veteran and bookshop proprietor near the University, told someone who asked for a book:

'Ah see it there on the shelf, but Ah canna be bothered going up for it today.'

The window-display at Bell & Bradfute's in Old Parliament Square was said to have been one of the unchanging features of the Edinburgh landscape. A native of the city, absent for many years in the Far East, wrote home for a book and described exactly which corner of which shelf it was on, with perfect confidence that it would be found there; and it was.

But there was another breed of

Edinburgh bookseller. There were a few young men of ideals and ambition, who saw books and magazines as the treasure-chest of knowledge and wisdom, essential for the advancement of the human race; and, more to the point, as prestigious business and a growth industry. These young men were going places in the golden age of Scottish literature. They took the plunge downhill from Old Town to New, set up their establishments in and around Princes Street and ordered such quantities of monthly and quarterly magazines from London that on 'magazine nights' (the last of the month) the mail coaches dragged in late, though driving six-in-hand instead of the usual four.

They spread out their new publications for inspection, to be browsed over by the reading public, says a diarist,

'with as much curiosity as a botanist might show in some rare specimens lately arrived from Van Diemen's Land.'

The *avant-garde* booksellers not only made money, they also founded dynasties. Their names in the Edinburgh directories of a hundred and sixty years ago are found in the yellow pages today. The first building in Princes Street, number ten, housed a prince of booksellers, Archibald Constable, who not only had the *Encyclopaedia Britannica* and the *Waverley* novels on his lists but also printed and sold the important Whig magazine, the *Edinburgh Review*. Constable crashed, but his name lives on.

From a house at number 17, a few doors away (now a John Menzies shop), came the Tory opposition monthly, *Blackwood's Magazine*. John Gibson Lockhart described William Blackwood's establishment as:

'the great lounging bookshop of the New Town of Edinburgh ... where various groups of loungers and literary dilettanti are engaged in looking at, or criticising among themselves, the publications just arrived by that day's coach. . . .'

Round the corner from Princes Street the house of Blackwood expanded and flourished and the descendants of William Blackwood are printing and publishing to the present day.

Round another corner, three half-centuries ago, the brothers Chambers slept under their counter, not being able to afford a night-watchman. They are now W.&R. Chambers the educational and encyclopaedia publishers. Up a stair at the back of the street lived John Bartholomew, a jobbing engraver who founded the famous map and atlas firm; across the street A.&C. Black, a pair of thrusters who made themselves responsible for various reference books and eventually blossomed out as the publishers of *Who's Who;* down the close an up-and-coming firm called Oliver & Boyd, specialists in academic and scientific textbooks ... did ever more extraordinary success stories of family concerns, more remarkable instances of father-to-son longevity, spring from one corner of a not-very-large city— all rising together, all engaged in the same sort of business?

Creech's bookshop, Edinburgh. Typical of the dusty, cramped and ill-lit premises in which Edinburgh literati browsed and John Menzies the first served his apprenticeship.

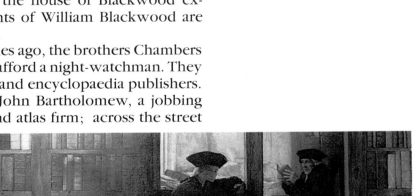

They were among the ninety-three booksellers of Edinburgh who at that period served a population of 130,000–more than there are today for a population of half a million. They were pioneers in what old James Thin described as:

'a calling of very high order, a civilising force in society.'

Their customers were the gentry and aristocracy and they were on familiar terms with Scott, de Quincey, Coleridge, Sidney Smith and Wordsworth, not to mention a swarm of best-selling authors of their day who are now forgotten. They made Edinburgh, in Lord Cockburn's words,

'a literary mart famous with strangers and the pride of its own citizens.'

Into the heart of that community in 1833 came John Menzies, aged

Below, right:
The Royal High School of Edinburgh, which migrated from its site near the Pleasance in the Old Town to a site under Calton Hill in 1829. This is the building known to John Menzies in his schooldays, 1816-1822.

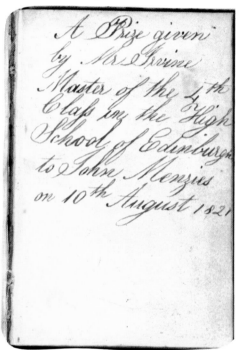

A memento of John Menzies's schooldays. The book which his schoolmaster presented to him on 10th August 1821.

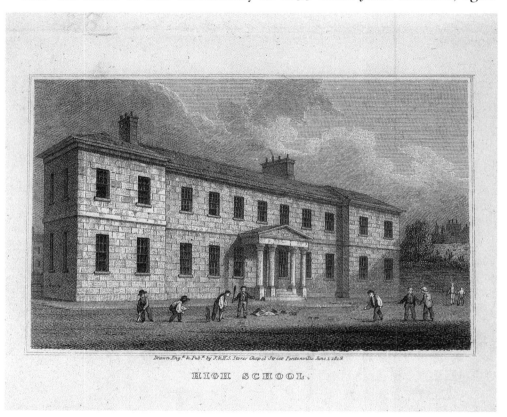

HIGH SCHOOL.

twenty-five. He was Edinburgh-born and bred, a former pupil of the Royal High School. (A memento of his schooldays is preserved in the archives of the company which bears his name; a prize book inscribed with the name of the donor, the schoolmaster Irvine, dated 10th August 1821.)

The Royal High School in the Old Town of Edinburgh (it moved to its Calton Hill site in 1829) was the cradle of education of scores of prominent Scots–classical scholars, mathematicians, politicians, divines, engineers, poets and painters, bankers and lawyers. John Menzies must have entered the school about twenty-five years after its most distinguished living pupil, Sir Walter Scott, left it.

From all one reads of the place, it was staffed by a brutal and sadistic mob of masters and daily floggings were not so much punishments for crime as part of the curriculum. Yet nearly all who passed through it looked back with affection. The thrashing of a whole class before lessons began, merely to put the boys in the right frame of mind, was regarded–at least in retrospect–as a really good joke. John Menzies in his old age spoke nostalgically of his schooldays and of childhood friends. One particular crony also made some stir in the world in future years: James Naysmith, inventor of the steam-hammer.

Between 1823 and 1830 John was an apprentice with Sutherland the bookseller in the Calton, close to Edinburgh Gaol (where St Andrew's House now stands). Of those years he rarely spoke. It wasn't easy to convey to a younger generation in more enlightened times the drudgery and discomfort of a bookseller's apprenticeship. Some of the do's and don'ts drawn up by Scottish firms for their employees give a general idea of it.

The apprentice arrived at the shop in time to wash the stairs and sweep

Below, left:
Dickensian impression of the world of commerce which John Menzies entered in 1823.

When John Menzies the first was a child, most Scottish celebrities found their way to the studios of Sir Henry Raeburn to have their portraits painted. This is Raeburn's head of Sir Walter Scott, giant of the romantic movement in literature.

the pavement and clean the window before he was called to prayers with the bookseller and his family at eight o'clock. During prayers he might expect to hear recited his misdeeds of the previous day. The Almighty would be invoked to give him strength to avoid repeating them. At nine the shop was opened and his day would be spent packing and unpacking books and delivering messages and parcels, apart from waiting on customers. If the bookseller was illiterate–quite a few of them were–he would also write the letters and keep the accounts and search for titles the customers wanted.

Each apprentice had to bring in his own supply of coals for the fire. In Edinburgh's bleak midwinter the wearing of topcoats was frowned on, but hats and neck-scarves might be kept on. Talking and smoking were forbidden. Calls of Nature were provided for, an alleyway or nearby garden being set aside for them, but no boy or young man left the premises without the bookseller's permission. Clothing at all times had to be funereal:

Rustic Slateford (now a suburb of Edinburgh) when the Union Canal and its aqueduct were new (1818) and people flocked to see the astonishing sight of ships crossing bridges and sailing through dry land.

'The staff will on no account disport themselves in raiment of bright colour, nor will they wear hose unless in good repair'–said the Ten Commandments of the firm of Ballantyne.

The apprentice had a whole hour for his dinner at noon, but was not expected to stop work while eating it. His day ended at nine p.m., when the shop shut. It might be later if a consignment of books was expected and the Highflyer coach was running behind time. Teenage boys worked this routine throughout the year, a fourteen-hour day, an eighty-four-hour week, with a day off on Sundays and on New Year's day.

If the young Menzies was typical of Edinburgh workers in those seven years, he would devote some of his spare time, and maybe the firm's time too, as he travelled on errands round the city, to observing a few of the miracles of technology that were being performed in Scotland's capital. In 1822, for example, the gas lamps came to Princes Street, bestowing 'a strong and beautiful light' and cutting down street crimes. In 1824 you could see the amazing sight of 'ships sailing through dry land' on the new Union canal. The same year Edinburgh's first fire brigade came to the streets, just in time to cope unsuccessfully with the fires of 1824 and 1825 which destroyed much of the Old Town. In 1826 excitement was centred on the Innocent Railway, from Edinburgh to Dalkeith, the first railway in Scotland, so named because throughout its history it was innocent of mishap.

For anyone in the book trade there was also literary and journalistic history to be seen in the making. Benjamin Disraeli, young, foppish and persuasive, canvassed the booksellers: he was trying to get another Tory magazine, the *Quarterly Review*, started. The first genuine Edinburgh newspaper got into its stride–the *Scotsman*, price sixpence (2½p). The Snowball Riots, a skirmish between university students and booksellers' apprentices, put the city in a state of panic and led to demands for the picturesque Old Town Guard (abolished in 1817) to be recalled.

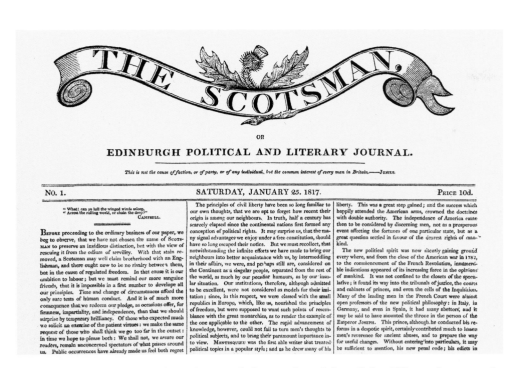

Part of page one, issue number one, of *The Scotsman*, the first genuine daily newspaper in Edinburgh. John Menzies the founder was nine years old when this newspaper appeared.

Sir Walter Scott finally admitted the authorship of the *Waverley* novels, clearing up the literary mystery of the age. John Menzies had had a glimpse of him years earlier, in a crowd watching some French prisoners breaking out of Edinburgh Castle and being rounded up in the morass along Princes Street. In 1826 he may have glimpsed him again, limping through Princes Street gardens to avoid the eyes of the citizens, for Sir Walter (along with other authors and several publishing companies) had been brought down in the collapse of the house of Constable under debts of a quarter of a million pounds.

The shock waves of that catastrophe travelled back and forth over the bookselling scene for years. Perhaps that awful demonstration of the underlying shakiness of the Scottish book world had some influence on the meditations of John Menzies's father. When his son came out of his apprenticeship he put him on board the London smack at the New Dock (now the Old East Dock) of Leith, with £10 in his pocket to tide him over until he found a job.

The young man's first regular employer was Charles Tilt of Fleet Street–a bookseller not quite in the top flight, but prominent enough to be a friend, and afterwards the chief executor, of the renowned Mr Hatchard of Piccadilly. Thanks to a memoir in the *Publisher's Circular* of April 1927, we know something about Tilt: that he was a good-natured, easy-going little man with black curly hair, though 'much burdened with home cares', whatever that meant. He sold books and published them and he went in for lithographs and (something of a novelty then) steel engravings.

His popular line, when his new Scottish assistant joined him, was picture-books of landscapes and figure studies. There was a vogue for Romneyesque portraiture, for prints of well-endowed society women flaunting their charms in neo-classical draperies. John Menzies must have had a hand in seeing titles like *Byron's Beauties* through the press; strong stuff for a strictly-brought-up Edinburgh boy.

All that Tilt's diary says about the association is:

'December 1831, Menzies as assistant. February 1833, Menzies left us'

—but there is word-of-mouth evidence that the two got on well together and that Tilt hinted at a partnership if only Menzies would stay with him. Afterwards, when John Menzies was in business on his own account, a correspondence developed which lasted until Tilt's death in 1861. Having printed, published and sold books for most of his life, Tilt ended up writing them. A description of travels in Egypt, where he had to go for his health, called *The Boat and the Caravan,* is inscribed to his friend John Menzies.

Of the great mass of people who grew up in the pre-photographic era, youthful portraits rarely survive. From later pictures and documents we can surmise that the young John Menzies, like most educated young Scots from the solid middle stratum of society, was open and manly in appearance, fastidious in manner and dress, puritanical by London standards, diligent and reliable in his work. He appears to have been one of those lucky people whom strangers instinctively take to. When he fell ill, soon after arriving in the metropolis, the doctor called in to attend him took him to his own house to recuperate–which argues something agreeable in John Menzies's character, or the doctor's, or both.

When he made friends, he kept them. His London experience lasted little more than a year, yet the contacts he made there at the age of twenty-three were among his friends when he died aged seventy-one. Some, no doubt, were useful to his business; but not all, for he recalled that

'while some have risen to a high position in the publishing world . . . others have remained in the same situation for forty years.'

He was among those destined to rise. From 1833, when he returned to Edinburgh, he operated independently and instantly made his mark. Through his correspondence and business dealings after that date we can see his personality taking shape.

Looking west down Princes Street, Edinburgh, from an uncompleted Waterloo Place, about 1818. The building on the right, with columns and clock towers, is the General Register House, built by the brothers Adam for the preservation of Scottish public records.

2

'Up a few steps'

'Up a few steps'

By December 1832 eight hundred lay dead in Edinburgh, the city hospitals were full and hundreds more of the citizens were enfeebled, poorly equipped to face a winter of Arctic severity; but the cholera epidemic, the worst in the capital's recorded history, had run its course.

Early in February 1833 John Menzies's father suddenly died (not, as far as we know, of the cholera) and his son came home. Now he had a step-mother and two sisters to support—an encumbrance to a young man on the threshold of a career, a powerful argument for taking a safe job with one of the old-established respectable booksellers who knew him.

Instead he set up in business for himself. Either way, the trade offered no spectacular rewards. To run a bookshop a young man needed capital and experience and then, with toil and sweat and luck, he might earn a steady living. Without luck the disagreeable possibilities were too dreadful to contemplate: ruin, disgrace, the debtor's gaol, lifelong beggary for self and dependants. In 1833 there was not even a poorhouse to go to.

John Menzies must have lived frugally in London. At least, he brought home rather more in his pocket than the ten sovereigns he took away. He travelled expensively in the mail-coach, two and a half days and nights in that ferocious winter, a journey he never forgot, though at that period it was considered a luxurious means of transport. Towards the end of the same year, having gathered some stock together, he rented a shop in Princes Street, the heart of the bookselling trade.

Property may have been going cheap just then in the stricken city. And on Princes Street, despite inducements, shopkeepers and private citizens had been slow to move into the plain Georgian-fronted buildings which formed a single line along the plainstanes, facing the marshy valley euphemistically called gardens. A painting by M. Egerton, about 1830, shows many 'Rooms to Let' above the timid scattering of taverns, bookshops, coach offices and pie-and-porter shops. John Menzies took number 61, 'up a few steps', as old James Thin remembered it, at the corner of Princes Street and Hanover Street. (The numbers don't correspond with those of the present day.)

Below: A letter from Mr Dickens, 1841. 'A tradition of the firm says that John Menzies and Charles Dickens were friends.'

Below right: A view of East Princes Street, Edinburgh, about the middle of last century, from an engraving by J. B. Ebsworth. Scott Monument (inaugurated 1846) on the right. Number 61, corner of Hanover Street, on extreme left.

Far right: Magazines of old Edinburgh. *Tait's* and *Blackwood's* were both published in Princes Street bookshops, close to Number 61.

It was quite a good address. His immediate neighbour was Tait of *Tait's Edinburgh Magazine,* an opposition journal to *Blackwood's* down the street at number 17. Mrs Grant of Laggan, the Highland diarist, lived a few doors along, as did Donaldson the publisher who made enough money out of his *Edinburgh Advertiser* and other ploys to endow the hospital school in Edinburgh which bears his name.

Within hailing distance were Tyndall Bruce the royal printer for Scotland and Henry Mackenzie, essayist and 'man of feeling'. Edmonston & Douglas, famous antiquarian book dealers, kept an eye on John Menzies from one side; Johnston & Hunter, specialists in religious books, from the other. When Dickens visited Edinburgh in 1841 he put up at the nearby Royal Hotel. (He had dealings with John Menzies and a tradition of the firm says the two were friends.) Campbell's Hotel, nearer still, became the Crown Hotel, where Tennyson wrote a poem while seated at its Princes Street bow-window.

A novice bookseller in that dignified environment might congratulate himself on being somewhere near the hub of the literary merry-go-round. He might also feel apprehension at the strength of the competition, but that was offset by promise of certain new outlets.

In the previous decade Edinburgh had set up a School of Arts, a sort of prototype Workers' Educational Association. In the space of five years it had generated Mechanics' Institutes, Philosophical Institutions and Mutual Improvement Associations all over the city—night-schools for reading and writing, in the main, despite their highflown titles. The Edinburgh philanthropists crowned their work in 1825 with the first Mechanics' Library which, within a generation, was the biggest in Britain.

Initially the booksellers had donated to these organisations out of their own stocks. By the time John Menzies arrived the organisations were mostly self-financing and their appetite for reading matter was voracious.

The newcomer to Princes Street was in his middle twenties, a precocious infant in the eyes of the booksellers around him. His assets were London contacts, courageous energy and a clear idea of his aims. London had shown

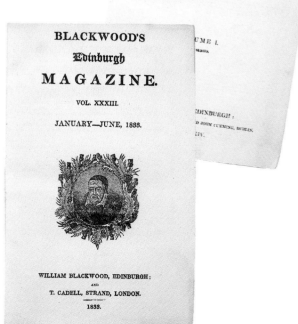

him that Edinburgh needed a wholesale distributor of books to the trade. London had taught him that the new magazines–*Cornhill, Good Words, Macmillan's*–were ready to build up their circulations in Scotland. From London he had learned that library shops were worth cultivating. (The library shop–there were twenty-three of them in Edinburgh alone–met the needs of a public which found the three-volume novels of Scott and Bulwer Lytton rather beyond its pocket at thirty shillings [£1.50] a time.)

All such branches of the literary business John Menzies undertook to promote, particularly the wholesaling. There had been wholesalers before, agents for London publishers, but their first priority was their own retail trade and in any conflict of interests the London publisher (as remote from Edinburgh as Tokyo is today) had to suffer. In Edinburgh there were good prospects for an agent uncommitted to local obligations. James Thin recalled that by 1835

'John Menzies was . . . agent for Charles Tilt & Co. (his former employer), whose Miniature Library was then much in demand. . . .

'He was widely known as agent for Messrs Chapman & Hall, then handling *Pickwick Papers* in the familiar green paper covers . . . Mr Menzies himself attended at the front counter and supplied demands from the trade. His business in time greatly extended. . . .'

Chapman & Hall gave him the disposal of all Dickens's work in the east of Scotland, an outpouring of best-sellers unbroken for thirty years. Bradbury & Evans appointed him their Scottish agent for the new satirical magazine *Punch*, price 3d (1¼p). It wasn't long before Edinburgh realised that if it wanted an out-of-the-way book, British or foreign, ancient or modern, Menzies's shop was the place to go for it.

Travellers in the Highlands, about the middle of the last century, noted as something remarkable that they saw crofters and shepherds reading Wordsworth and Thackeray and that they found copies of the *London Journal* and the *Family Herald* in lonely bothies and gamekeepers' cottages. Rural readers had John Menzies to thank for that phenomenon.

In a survey of bookselling trends, 1859, *The Bookseller* drew attention to the 'rapidly increasing business' of the firm. Compared with the meteoric history of some enterprises when Railway Mania was at its height, it was steady rather than sensational. 'Cash received in business was very small' according to the founder's little notebook in 1833– but that wasn't a full year. Receipts for 1834 were £926, of which perhaps £100 was profit. In the next two years turnover doubled, in the next four it doubled again (£3,925 in 1840); and over the next ten years it doubled once more (£8,148 in 1850).

Menzies appears to have run the shop single-handed until 1837, when he hired a clerk named Duncan Macnab at £30 a year and engaged three apprentices. Ten years after that he employed at least two clerks, a porter and a string of apprentices. Notations such as 'Dismissed for thieving' stand against some of the names. The proprietor was merciless on dishonesty.

In *Gray's Edinburgh Directory* for 1834-5 John Menzies is described as Bookseller, Stationer & Printseller. He also published books and engravings and sold the *Scotsman* newspaper–a daring experiment, for newspapers were not generally on sale to the public. You had to get them by subscription,

'The new satirical magazine *Punch*, price 3d.' An issue of 1842. John Menzies was sole distributor in Scotland.

direct from the publisher. It was a landmark in journalism when, in 1836, Edinburgh's *Evening Post* was 'cried' on the streets by a man with a trumpet, along with the ballads and political broadsheets and the half-legible accounts of the latest murder.

At number 61 you could buy your newspaper; also books, magazines, inks, pens, account books and office equipment. Some of the books bore the Menzies imprint, and some he brought out in collaboration with other booksellers–Charles Tilt, Marcus Ward, Simpkin Marshall. Little guides to regions of Scotland and scenes and descriptions of places made familiar by Sir Walter Scott were the earliest lines. In his old age John Menzies smiled over them, saying how warmly they had been admired in their day, how 'they wouldn't be thought much of now'. But some will disagree. The black-and-white, steel-engraved, gilt-edged landscapes, about the size of a picture postcard, are full of charm and Gothic romance. Indeed, they anticipated the pictorial viewcards on which, starting half a century later, Mr Valentine of Dundee built his fortune. Collected in mid-Victorian albums of views, they must have facilitated many an accidental brushing of finger-tips as the pages were turned in the drawing-room, and must have helped many a flirtation along.

In our own times, when the house of Menzies appealed for material for a museum, quantities of *Views on Cards, Picturesque Sketches* and the like came to light in a condition which suggested they had been lovingly preserved and handed down like heirlooms.

A plain paper-covered school jotter served John Menzies as Publishing Book. In it are recorded the sales of four sets of *Vignette Views* in silky tartan covers. The four sets were in print for four years and sold 90,000 copies. Overheads must have been high, for the total profit was only £232.

The rest of the publishing list tells even less of a success story. Captain Charles Gray wrote to the publisher to thank him for his 'vain efforts' to procure a sale for his *Lays and Lyrics*. No one seems to have recognised the author of *Songs of the Rail* as a poet, or even as a forerunner of McGonagall:

'Right across the six-foot way,
One huge bulk, engine and tender lay,
While the wailing hiss of steam took the air
By fits, like the low dull tone of despair. . . .'

The same dull tone applied to *The True Python's Oracle,* a phrase-book for Continental travellers, which opened with the useful question: 'Is the lady in the family way?'–it sold two copies only. Against the last entry for it in the Publishing Book appears a sad little note:

'1862. The stock of the work having remained on the shelves for twenty-five years, and no sale, has been used for waste paper, the parties to whom it belonged having been dead for a long period.'

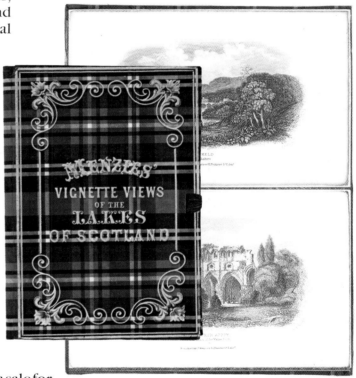

Vignette Views, an early Menzies publishing venture. 'The founder recalled how warmly they had been admired.'

John Menzies's most noteworthy publishing venture involved two young authors who claimed a brilliant ancestry: John Sobieski Stolberg Stuart, alias the Chevalier Stuart, alias the Count of Albany; and his brother Charles Edward Stuart. Sentimental Jacobites accepted them as grandsons of Bonnie Prince Charlie and as rightful king and rightful heir presumptive respectively of Great Britain. They settled in Scotland, where they had a large reservoir of ancient sympathies to draw on and where they were invited to some of the best houses.

In 1843, when the centenary of the Young Pretender's adventure was approaching, the brothers asked John Menzies to bring out their new book, *Costumes of the Clans*.

John Sobieski Stolberg Stuart
(1796?-1872)

Right: Autograph letter from the Chevalier Stuart, with formidable signature and sample of the 'fine crimson cloath'.

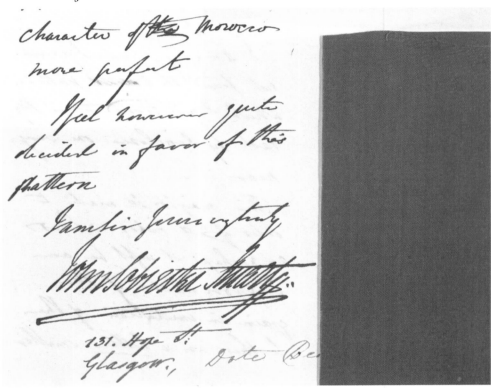

It was a troublesome business, not made easier by John Sobieski Stuart's obsession with ceremony and protocol and his condescending arrogance. The letter-franking privileges which went along with the brothers' free board and lodging in various ducal castles allowed them to write long letters by every post, changing their instructions, asking the impossible, confusing the situation, saying one thing and meaning another and dismissing protests with regal indifference. Their missives were delivered in a florid scrawl, with much underscoring of words and an Elizabethan signature which wandered all over the page.

At the binding stage John Sobieski decided he wanted more of a coffee-table format:

'The Chevalier . . . begs you to communicate to Messrs Ballantyne & Hughes [printers] his wish that *this size* should be adopted, with the observation that though the *page* is larger the *number of pages* will be *proportionately diminished* and therefore *no increase of expenditure* incurred. . . .'

Publisher and printer struggled on with *Costumes of the Clans* under fusillades of rebukes for their 'untimely procrastination' and a hailstorm of arbitrary and ambiguous last-minute demands:

'The Chevalier requests that *all* the copies may be bound in *fine crimson cloath* only . . . (but) a few shall be half-bound, that is with crimson morocco back and corners. . . .

'It is particularly requested that three copies may be furnished as soon as possible for the Emperor of Austria, the King of Bavaria and the Archduke Stephen . . . that Mr Menzies will give the Chevalier timely warning . . . that he may make arrangements with the Prussian and Austrian Consuls for the transmission of the Volumes under the *Royal and Imperial Seals* . . .

Charles Edward Stuart (1799?-1880)

Left: 'In the highest Style of Art.' Two of the thirty colour plates which illustrated *Costumes of the Clans.*

this to be done in London, as the Hull direct water line will of course be *stopt* by the freezing of the Elbe. . . .'

And so on and so forth and so to publication day. Who were these larger-than-life 'royals' who made John Menzies's life a misery for about eighteen months in the middle 1840s? Unlikely to have been 'royals' at all, is history's verdict.

They first appeared in Scotland in 1818, aged about twenty-two and nineteen respectively, though at different times they gave themselves different ages. Before that they had been in London, learning Gaelic, and before that, according to their own testimony, had fought under Napoleon at Leipzig, Dresden and Waterloo. They had grown up believing themselves to be the sons of a half-pay naval lieutenant named Allen, who was understood to be the offspring of Admiral Allen, a distant connection of the Hay family of Erroll. But in their early teens (they said) a former royal physician had whispered a secret to them: that their father was not the son of Admiral

Allen; that he was the only son of Bonnie Prince Charlie, a son the genealogists never knew about because as a baby he'd been smuggled out of Naples and aboard Admiral Allen's flagship, for fear of a political kidnapping.

The brothers called themselves Allan (sic), then Allan-Hay, then Stuart-Allan-Hay, then Hay-Allan-Stuart and finally Stuart. In 1822, when George IV made his state visit to Scotland, Sir Walter Scott saw the elder brother, in his tartan phillibegs and badge of High Constable (a hereditary Erroll appointment), being presented to the King.

The old Jacobite patriarchs—Lord Lovat, the Earl of Moray, the Marquess of Bute—sent for them, saw them and were conquered. The brothers did resemble some portraits of the Young Pretender and they certainly had the Stuart arrogance and love of finery. They had the Gaelic too. They wrote birthday odes to each other and flattering poems to their hosts and pseudo-Scottish narrative poems, *Lays of Ancient Caledonia* and suchlike. They started another Ossian controversy with their book *Vestiarium Scoticum*, supposedly a sixteenth-century work they had discovered, a history of 'ye chieffe Hieland and bordour clannes'. Scholars ridiculed it, but it had gone down well with the Scottish nobility. *Costumes of the Clans* was to be a companion-piece to that work. While the book was in preparation the brothers continued travelling about, visiting Prague, Vienna and Munich where, it was said, no one thought to question their exalted status. Back in Scotland, they wrote to John Menzies from Inveraray Castle, Kames Castle in Bute and Beauly House near Dingwall. They built themselves a moss cabin beside the Findhorn river and from there they moved to a lodge which Lord Lovat gave them on an islet in the Beauly river. They invariably wore the full Highland dress with many sashes, ribbons and orders. Estate workers at Beauly gathered on Sundays to see the brothers rowed to church, preceded by banners and a personal piper and followed by a retinue. Local gentry kissed hands, the ladies curtseyed and all retreated backwards from the presence.

Costumes of the Clans, Imperial folio size, came out in June 1844, price six guineas to pre-publication subscribers, seven and a half guineas to others. It contained thirty colour plates 'in the highest Style of Art' and also observations on fashion, Highland history, Gaelic songs and the wool trade. The *Dictionary of National Biography* calls the production sumptuous and the pictures grotesque. It was indeed the perfect sequel to the *Vestiarium*: spurious, plagiaristic and an insult to scholarly intelligence.

Although the Duke of Sutherland and the Duke of Leeds headed the subscription list and Queen Victoria accepted a copy for her library, it seems to have sold only about fifty of the ninety copies printed. (It came out fifty years later in a cheap edition, but made no stir.) The brothers were still in Scotland, still enjoying the kind of adulation appropriate to the reincarnations of a pair of Bonnie Prince Charlies, when an article by Professor Skene in the *Quarterly Review* (June 1847) completely demolished their claims and exposed them as frauds.

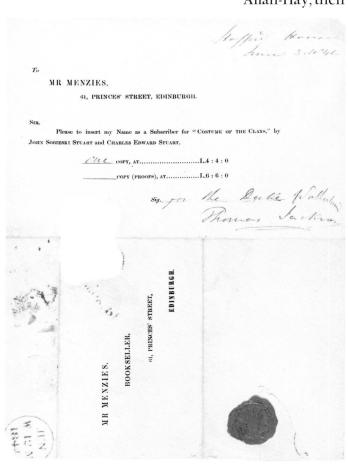

Above: Order form for *Costumes of the Clans*. 'The book proved a heavy loss.'

The rebirth of hopes for the house of Stuart has little to do with the growth of the house of Menzies, but the episode did shed light on the founder's character. When the most prominent people in Scotland received the new Pretenders, when ordinary citizens believed in them, when grovelling flunkeyism was the rule in dealing with gentlemen of rank, let alone royalty, John Menzies ignored his clients' pretensions. He gave the self-styled Chevaliers no title, no special form of address, not even an 'esquire'. He showed them common politeness and perhaps an unusual degree of patience. He treated them from the first like simple authors, which they were; and at the last like defaulting customers, which they turned out to be.

One matter which John Menzies didn't hurry over was the matter of wedlock. He was nearly forty when, in 1845, he married a Miss Rossie Marr. Her father was a merchant of Leith. They went to London for a fortnight's honeymoon, which cost him £34 (the expenses are carefully itemised).

In several ways it was a memorable year for him. He issued the first of his monthly Book Lists to retailers, a catalogue of stock which came out regularly thereafter until the 1940s; supplemented from May 1914 onwards by Menzies's Weekly Notes to the trade.

From his shop front in that same year he saw the navvies digging up Princes Street gardens, making way for Steam. The first long-distance train out of Edinburgh, to London in 1846, was an object of significance to the future of the business, though he would hardly have been aware of that.

A painting of John Menzies, done in old age, shows him candid, mellow and good-humoured-looking. Portraits are notoriously poor guides to character. A different picture emerges from his correspondence of younger days–but letters too can be misleading. They portray a man of driving ambition and obdurate self-will, making his way in a pitiless world. Business acquaintances paid tribute to his honesty, sound judgment and skill in managing limited resources. A good education, a healthy physique, a fondness for work and some knowledge of the trade beyond Edinburgh gave him advantages. Had you asked what epitaph he would like for his tomb, he might have answered: 'I paid my way'. He prided himself on paying cash for everything; yet this was a period when all but the most firmly-established booksellers lived on credit and bills of exchange, on account of the capital outlay and slow returns inherent in the business.

If stern moralists have a fault it is usually self-righteousness. John Menzies must have been a hard man to borrow money from: while hounding his debtors he couldn't resist lecturing them on their human frailties. To Ballantyne the printer in July 1850, following a request for the loan to be repaid:

'. . . I am certainly not a little surprised that you have sent me no answer, as this was no ordinary claim but *borrowed money* which, from every feeling of character and credit as an honest man and a gentleman you are bound to repay. . . . That this was your own feeling the annexed quotation amply proves. . . .'

Below: Facsimile of the first (1845) monthly Book List sent out by John Menzies.

JANUARY 1845.   ISSUED MONTHLY.

A LIST

OF

NEW BOOKS AND NEW EDITIONS

SOLD BY

J. MENZIES,

61 PRINCE'S STREET, EDINBURGH.

ARCHÆOLOGICAL ALBUM, No. 1. Post 4to, Numerous Woodcuts and Five Plates, to be continued every alternate Month. 5s.

Byron's Corsair, 48 pages, sewed in a Handsome Wrapper (Clarke's Home Library, No. 7.) 4d.
Ball Room Annual for 1845. 1s.

CHAPMAN AND HALL'S MONTHLY SERIES OF NOVELS. Post 8vo, to be continued Monthly. Part. I. commencing Mount Sorel, or the Heiress of the De Veres. 3s.
Countess Faustina, (The), (No. 45 of Clarke's Cabinet Series.) 2s.
Cruickshank's, (George), Table Book, No. 1. Post 8vo, to be continued Monthly, 1s.

DICKENS' CHIMES. A Goblin Story, with Plates, fcap. cloth, gilt edges. 5s.
.... Christmas Carol. Tenth Edition. 5s.

Female Blue Beard, (The), by Eugene Sue, 12mo, cloth. 3s.

Gleig's Sermons for Advent, 12mo, bds. 5s.

Herrick's Hesperides, Vol. II. (Clarke's Cabinet Series.) 2s.

Illustrated Shakspere (The), Re-issue in Weekly Numbers, 6d.; and Monthly Parts, 2s. 6d.

–and John Menzies goes on to throw back in Ballantyne's teeth the pathetically optimistic promises he had made.

It was the principle of the thing, not the size of the debt, that Menzies worried about. He paid on the nail, and had no patience with those who didn't. To Alex Scott, bookseller of Peebles, June 1846:

'Sir, I have repeatedly sent in a small account of 4/6½ (about 23p)...I do not know what your motives are in withholding payment of an account justly due but as such conduct appears to me unfair and unhandsome I am determined to let you see that payment, if not willingly made, can be compelled by law, though the doing so may cause some little trouble and expense to myself. . . .'

There is acrimonious correspondence with Blackwood about a Bible–a matter which might have been settled over the counter, for the shop was only a few yards along the street. There's an encounter with the Aberdeen bookseller Wyllie about a book he asked Menzies to send him and then found he didn't want ('It is perfectly unreasonable your keeping this Book for months...I could have sold it to the Trade half a dozen times'). There is a

Right: 'Acrimonious correspond-ence.' A set of mottled leather-bound volumes in the firm's archives contains copies of the founder's outgoing business letters. This Letter Book covers the period 1844-1856.

thundering reaction to what Menzies was beginning to regard as threats to his territory. To James MacLeod, Glasgow, November 1845:

'With regard to what you say of Dickens's new book, I am perfectly aware that you have solicited orders for it in Edinburgh, but you had better beware, because for any injury you can do to my sales here I can retaliate threefold in Glasgow. . . .'

And defaulters needn't think to escape by emigrating to the ends of the earth. To George McWilliam Esq., Edinburgh, July 1850:

'Dear Sir, A letter which I sent to your nephew Mr James McWilliam has been returned to me with a writing on it, stating that he has sailed for Australia. He has done so leaving a debt . . .'

–which John Menzies proposes to collect by writing round the young man's relations and friends.

One way and another, and allowing that business people of that era had to express themselves forcibly if they didn't want to be trodden on, the bookseller at number 61 could hardly have been the most popular man in Princes Street. No glimmer of humour, no sign of what one might call the

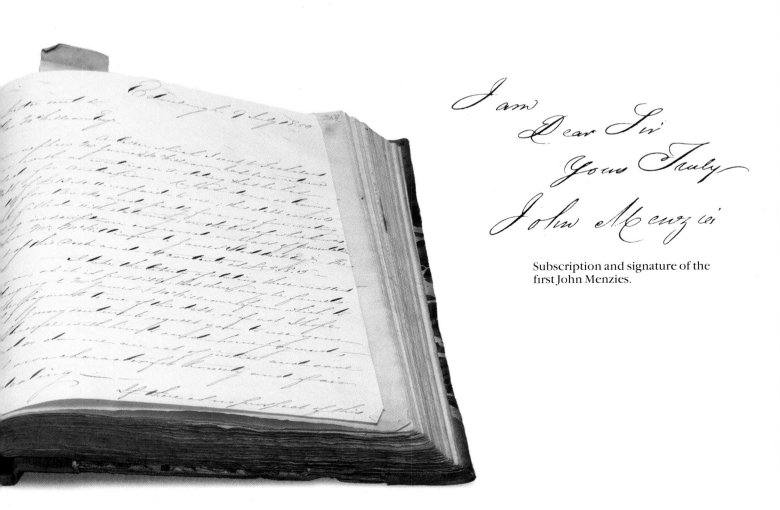

Subscription and signature of the first John Menzies.

The Royal Institution of Edinburgh (now the Royal Scottish Academy), with Castle behind. From Menzies's *Vignette Views of Edinburgh*, 1837.

flexible response, enliven his business letters. They indicate a sense of superiority and personal pride which some people, in a tradesman, must have resented. It was still the green-baize-apron era for publishers and booksellers and they were supposed to let a decent interval elapse before rendering an account; to render it with due deference and many apologies for mentioning the matter; and to express a fawning gratitude if a customer was so gracious as to take notice of it. They were not supposed to write to personages who hobnobbed with emperors in the manner in which John Menzies started writing not long after the publication of *Costumes of the Clans*.

'John Sobieski Stuart. Sir, Your letter dated Vienna, 31st January, was delivered to me. You say that you transmitted to me an intimation of your intention to quit Prague, no such intimation reached me, but I beg to say that I have written to the address you gave me three different times, requesting payment of the account rendered to you of £25.16.0, also to your Brother for payment of the account rendered to him of £9.–.8, to none of which applications has any reply been given by you or him.

'If you will refer to your account you will see that part of it is for six copies of *Costumes of the Clans* delivered to parties by your Order. If your Brother will refer to his account he will see that part of it is for two copies in like manner delivered to his Order. A full account of the sale of the Book cannot be made up till you and he pay for your copies, and I have now again to request that you will do so.

'I may add that the Book has proved a heavy loss to those who were at the expense of producing it, the amount of sales not having nearly covered the outlay, and as the eight copies supplied to you and your Brother amount to a considerable sum . . . I hope you will see the propriety and justice of speedily paying for them.'

It's not likely that the debts were discharged. The two 'pretenders' had been insolvent for years. Yet they managed to live on hospitality and hand-outs from European royalty and from Scottish loyalists who still believed in them. On their visits to London they were among the sights, particularly when engaged on their arcane researches at the British Museum where they sat, flamboyantly attired and wearing swords and spurs, at a special table equipped for them with coroneted pens and ink-bottles. The thought of it must have driven John Menzies wild.

John Sobieski Stuart and Charles Edward Stuart died at their Lovat lodge, the former in 1872 and the latter in 1880. They are buried under a monument at Eskadale, a short distance upstream from Beauly. The monument is florid, as their lives were; and in the spirit of the lies and deceptions they practised the inscription gives wrong dates for their births.

3

'A very striking change'

'A very striking change'

Waverley station, Edinburgh, was begun in 1836 and the first line went northward from it, through a tunnel under St Andrew Square to Leith. The line to Glasgow, through Princes Street gardens, was opened in 1846. This picture, taken during the 1890s, shows NBR (North British Railway) trains outside the station. Mr Menzies's shop is out of the picture, on the left, among the Princes Street buildings in the background.

Edinburgh shopkeepers of 1846 no longer shut their windows against dust and dirt from the railway excavations–they shut them against sparks and smoke instead. A railway line for Leith went under St Andrew Square. Another, for Glasgow, ran parallel with Princes Street through the drained swamp of the gardens. A third, for London, skirted the walls of the Palace of Holyroodhouse. Daily passenger trains, carrying also books and magazines, left London at six a.m. and arrived in Edinburgh at ten p.m., an astonishing acceleration of the rate of travel. Eight years earlier the journey had taken four times as long.

On the eastern side of Scotland, by 1846, there were railways to Stirling and Perth. By 1847 they were all over Fife. By 1848 the line had reached Montrose and in 1849 it was in Aberdeen.

Initial reaction was unfavourable. City folk feared that the smoke of the locomotives would obscure the sky, their flames set all the buildings on fire and their noise stampede the horses. Border tweed manufacturers were convinced that the grime from the trains affected the wool of sheep; and dairy farmers reported a sharp decline in milk yields. It soon appeared that, far from being the curse of mankind, Steam promoted almost everyone's interests, even the horse-dealers', since carriage traffic to and from the stations more than made up for the decline in the long-distance stage-coach services. The railways increased the demand for virtually every commodity, including reading matter.

John Menzies, in the intervals between making up his catalogues and writing irritable letters to clients, could look out in both directions and see main stations with huge hotels beside them: the North British to the east, the Caledonian to the west, each named for the railway company which owned it; and his shop stood midway between them. If he had foreseen his future role as a supplier of railway travellers' needs he could hardly have chosen a better base than number 61 Princes Street. Possibly, being a forward-looking man, he *did* foresee something of the kind. Possibly he recognised that, as Sidney Smith said, the British would want to read while on train journeys, if only to protect themselves from conversation; that every sensible person boarding a train would, in R. S. Surtees's words,

'have at least a newspaper in hand, in case tiresome people *will* talk–a purpose for which railway travelling was never intended.'

The name of John Menzies was one day to be synonymous with station bookstalls, at least throughout Scotland, but he didn't invent them. That important amenity appeared in the wake of the refreshment room in the dawn of the locomotive era. The man who claimed to have opened the first proper bookstall, not counting the rudimentary stalls set out by some of the railway companies themselves, was Horace Marshall, founder of a firm which eventually became part of the Menzies empire. That was in 1840, at Fenchurch Street station in London.

The prototype bookstall was a cheap wooden structure about the shape and size of a kitchen dresser, with the stock displayed on racks and the stall-holder standing inside it like a Punch-and-Judy man. Then it became an open wooden box with a counter. From that it evolved into a unit with shelves and cupboards and a padlock to protect the stock. As time went by the bookstall acquired a roof and, at larger stations, a cubby-hole at the side which served as an office. Woolworth's are generally credited with having invented 'open display', but F. W. Woolworth had not been heard of when the first railway bookstalls offered the same kind of layout.

By contemporary accounts most bookstalls of the 1840s were about as respectable as brothels. 'Centres of vice' and 'haunts of undesirables' were among the milder descriptions that reformers applied to them. They were mostly staffed by crippled or invalided railway employees among whom, before they adjusted themselves to the unprecedented speeds of trains, casualties were numerous. Their wares, we're informed, consisted of

'cheap French novels of the shadiest class and mischievous trash of every description.'

A writer to *The Times* wanted to know if the railway companies were bent on undermining the nation's morals by allowing 'such a vile book as Byron's *Don Juan* to pollute their stalls' and another correspondent alleged that

'persons who would be ashamed to be found reading certain works at home have asked for publications of the worst character at railway bookstalls.'

What with pickpockets, loose women and salacious reading matter, the bookstalls made quite a lot of the news they sold. It was as though the British, needing something to grouse about and finding most of their railway fears unjustified, launched their discontent on the bookstalls. Decades later, a veteran *Glasgow Herald* reporter recalled how the editor, when short of a leading article, would tell him to do 'something biting about the bookstalls'– the deplorable ruffians in charge of them, the disreputable characters who hung round them, the 'unmitigated rubbish' (flashy novels, bottles of beer, sandwiches and jars of sweets) which was on sale.

Railway conversation, or the lack of it, was a popular subject for cartoonists. This one, from *Punch*, 8th September 1883, shows a dejected "Wilkins" who has been nagged since the journey began by the lady opposite. Sympathetic passenger, from behind his newspaper: "Mother-in-law?" Wilkins: "Yes." SP: "Got just such 'nother at home." (They commiserate with each other at the next buffet.)

On 1st November 1848 (known to historians as the 'Year of Revolutions') a Mr W.H. Smith accomplished his own revolution. A very young man, and in defiance of his father's gloomy predictions, he took on the lease of the Euston station bookstall from the London & North-western Railway Company. Smith's were already an established newspaper-and-periodical firm, more than fifty years old and employing more than three hundred people. They ran a lending library and they owned reading rooms in London's Strand, where you could see the daily papers and scores of magazines for a subscription of one and a half guineas a year (£1.57).

For his crusade against squalid bookstalls and pernicious literature, Mr W.H. Smith became known along the L.&N.W.R. routes as the North-western Missionary. After him came John Menzies. The two concessionaires, one in England and one in Scotland, introduced top hats, frock coats and polite manners and made their bookstalls into oases of dignity and serenity amid the bustle of platform arrival and departure.

Stirling station, early in the present century. A typical Scottish provincial station, opened 1846, with fretted eaves, station clock and (from 1857 onwards) John Menzies bookstall.

John Menzies was not even first on the bookstall scene in Scotland. Vague reports from the expansion era of Steam tell of pioneers like Thomas Smith of Elgin (at Elgin station) and David Robertson of Perth (at Dunkeld station, opened 1849, probably the first station in Scotland to have a bookstall) and an unnamed entrepreneur who obtained permission to sell magazines in the men's lavatory at St Andrews station, 'provided he did not interfere with the normal business of the premises'. About this time the name of Thomas Murray enters Scottish bookstall history–a name enshrined for more than a century in the vest-pocket miniature *Murray's Diary*, price one penny. The *Diary*, so-called because it had a calendar with space for microscopic notes on its middle pages, gave train times to and from every station and was one of the simplest and most effective timetables ever devised.

No reliable timetable exists of John Menzies's move into the bookstall business, but it seems that his first agreement to rent platform stances was signed with the Scottish Central Railway in February 1857. He took the sites at Bridge of Allan, Perth and Stirling for £10, £25 and £15 a year respectively. (An article in *Chambers's Journal* said that Perth and Stirling were the first actually opened, in May 1857, and that Bridge of Allan followed in July.)

In the same year he acquired Waterloo (Aberdeen) and Keith stations from the Great North of Scotland Railway for £6 a year apiece. By 1859 he had taken sole rights on all the North-east of Scotland's lines between Perth and Aberdeen for £30 a year, all stations between Perth and Ladybank (Edinburgh, Perth & Dundee Railway) for £5 a year and the Scotland Street station in Edinburgh, which served rural Fife via the Granton-Burntisland floating bridge, the first train-ferry in the world.

He offered for Waverley (Edinburgh) station when W.H. Smith & Son's lease expired in 1857, but the bid was turned down. He persisted–the place was on his own doorstep and doubtless he considered it his by right–and the saga illustrates how the commercial pace was quickening and how pressure forced the prices up. Originally he offered a rent of £70; Thomas Murray of Glasgow offered more; W.H. Smith & Son offered to *buy* the Waverley bookstall; but all were rejected. That was in 1857. Five years later Menzies succeeded with a bid of £180. The written agreement of 1862 survives. It gives him the right to sell 'books, pamphlets and newspapers' every lawful day (that is, every weekday) between 6.15 a.m. and 10.15 p.m. In return he promises that his employees shall be 'in apparent good health, clean in their persons and apparel, and civil to passengers' and that he will not sell any book 'objectionable in its moral character or tendency'.

Waverley was his, but after five years he had to pay £400 to renew the lease. For a few more years bookstall rents moved up exponentially: it was the heyday of the private railway companies. Bookstalls remained desirable properties for another half-century and then, around 1930, they slumped.

In the boom years the railways, proliferating at a speed which seems incredible now, transformed the Scottish and English countryside into what a superannuated coachman called 'a gridiron of rails'. Someone heard a snatch of conversation between a prospector's surveyor and an inhabitant of Dolphinton in the wilds of Lanarkshire:

"Is there much traffic here?"

"Od, there's an auld wifie comes ower the hill wi' a basket o' ribbons now and then, but that's all the traffic I ken o'."

It didn't stop Dolphinton getting its branch line and it was the same story everywhere. The prospectors were all over the place, the navvies and the rails came after them, the junctions and sidings grew apace. A bookstall operator had to move rapidly to keep up with them. It was a time for swift decisions, for bargaining and for marking out spheres of influence. At an early stage John Menzies attempted a deal with his rival Thomas Murray, offering him £10 a year more than he paid for each of his bookstalls in the east of Scotland and promising not to interfere in the west . . . but Murray hung back.

Menzies must often have had to ask himself, as he stretched his finances to the limit, the questions which go together in most expanding commercial operations: "Can I afford to? Can I afford *not* to?" In 1859, for the first time in his career, he applied to his bank for a loan. Evidently they considered him to be on a viable course. They lent him £9000 without

Cover of the famous *Murray's Diary*, price one penny, 'the neatest little timetable ever devised'. Rail travellers for more than a hundred years were familiar with it.

demur. (He increased his overdraft to £11,000 in 1871 and to £14,000 in 1877. His successors gradually reduced the figure to nil.)

His principal railway landlords were the Caledonian and the North British companies (afterwards L.M.&S. and L.&N.E. Railways). He took over the Caledonian sites in big batches. In January 1867, for example, he secured all the leases which fell vacant that year except that of Carstairs Junction, which came within Thomas Murray's ambit. Other companies released their bookstall concessions in penny numbers and he collected them one by one over a long period. It was not until 1911, in his two sons' reign, that the firm picked up the last station on the West Highland line at Spean Bridge; and not until 1918 that it added the last two Fife stations, Largo and Lundin Links, to its list. (But Menzies's never erected bookstalls at those places.)

The east and north of Scotland were acquired fairly painlessly. In Glasgow and the south-west John Menzies met fierce competition. The firm gained a foothold with a bookstall at Glasgow Central in 1881; the founder did not quite live to see it. Every bid for another mainline Glasgow station, Queen Street, failed. It fell into the firm's hands only in 1946, when John Menzies & Company Limited took over the whole business of the long-time lessee, Robert Graham. For many years the stations on the old Glasgow & South-western lines eluded capture. It was a landmark in company history

The name of Menzies first came before the public at the railway bookstalls, and first of all at the small stations of central Scotland. By the time these pictures were taken, the bookstalls had become a prominent, eye-catching feature of Platform One. Below: Oban and right: Alloa, about ninety years ago.

when Fairlie station on the Clyde coast was conquered in May 1883.

Two bookstalls, both in Glasgow, were never offered for. One was at Bridgeton Cross, which presumably the firm didn't want. The other was at Lenzie, which went by tradition to the stationmaster's widow.

Whenever Menzies built or took over a bookstall, a new era was proclaimed for that locality. Typical of the unsolicited tributes for a generation or more was this paragraph in the *East Cumberland News* in 1887, referring to the firm's first venture south of the Border:

'Since Mr Menzies became tenant of the Carlisle station bookstalls a very striking change has passed over those establishments and over the literary services of the station generally. The stalls are now furnished with large, handsome and varied supplies, not only of popular books but of those of permanent value. . . . Mr Menzies's resources enable him to make periodic changes which offer a constant and enticing choice. The variety of periodicals and newspapers is also greater and every train is waited upon with well-provided newsboys. . . .'

John Menzies appointed managers to keep the bookstalls and deal with platform custom. In country towns, where the railway station was the gossip-exchange, marriage mart and hall of leisure for half the population, business could be considerable. In quiet districts the bookstall manager (or manageress, for women were often employed) might have charge of

"Striking changes," a newspaper said, "have passed over the literary services of the stations." By the 1890s the Menzies bookstalls were spread over the railway map of Scotland from Dundee (left) in the east to Hamilton (below) in the west.

"Doon the watter" in the *Guinevere*, pride of the old Clyde paddle steamers. John Menzies provided basket-boy services on many of the excursion boats and ferry links among the islands and resorts of the Firth of Clyde.

A Menzies "basket boy" in his uniform. He acted as a per-ambulating mini-bookstall for passengers in trains which stopped at his platform.

several stances miles apart, and travel from one to the other by train two or three times a week. Menzies's man at Elgin, for example, also controlled Lossiemouth and Craigellachie stations.

On a big station, especially where the refreshment-room proprietor's charter required trains to make mandatory stops of twenty minutes and passengers had little to do but browse at the bookstall, the manager's job was made up of periods of boredom alternating with periods of frenetic activity. He would have one or two assistants and also a team of newsboys or 'basket boys', with trays strapped to their shoulders, to serve the passengers in trains which stopped only briefly. Well into our own times the platform newsboy was part of the station *mise-en-scène;* very much a part of Menzies history. It was a part-time occupation for school-children, who could serve the arriving long-distance night trains first thing in the morning and the arriving day trains after school in the evening.

Menzies's boys were systematically recruited and trained. They carried identity cards and wore metal identification tallies on their wrists. Sometimes you would see the basket boy, with hurriedly replenished stock, boarding the train he had just served; it was his duty, if no more trains were expected for a while, to voyage down the line, jump off and sell his wares in some other place and return to his headquarters on the next convenient train.

Before John Menzies established his bookstalls on the Clyde steamers he put basket boys on board to tour the lounges and upper decks, offering periodicals and miscellaneous goods to the passengers. (At holiday times they wore straw boaters and ribbons with the boat's name on them.) You might also have met the boy in the station hotels, selling morning and evening papers. When Aberdeen's Palace Hotel burned down in 1941 it was noted that for many years John Menzies's had paid £1 a year for the privilege of sending a boy with newspapers through the public rooms twice a day.

During rush hour at a big railway terminus poachers moved in among the basket boys. A letter of the 1880s to the *Edinburgh Evening News* protested against

'these repeated floggings of newspaper boys for trying to earn a living by

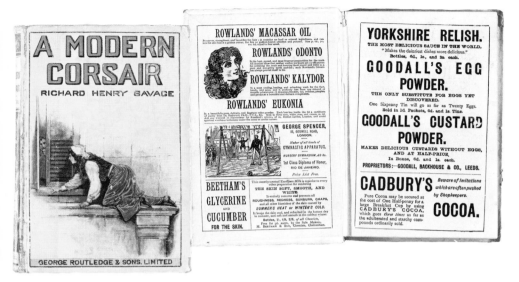

selling their wares at Waverley station.'

Pointing out that the 'little ragged fellows' were performing a service, the official newsboy invariably being at the wrong end of the platform when you wanted him, the writer asked:

'What law or bye-law authorises Sheriff Hamilton to inflict the brutal penalty of the lash upon these little workers? What must be the emotions in the hearts of these little merchants, what must be their estimate of this as a Christian land as they feel themselves driven, perhaps, by fear of the lash at home to dispose of their papers, and driven from doing so by similar fears instilled by "law and order"?'

The railway company would have argued that cruelty was really kindness. Accidents to newsboys, falling between platform-edge and carriage-step or racing into the path of a locomotive while crossing the line, were not infrequent.

When John Menzies promoted his Bridge of Allan manager to the Stirling bookstall he suggested looking for a successor in the shape of 'some young respectable woman who might employ herself with her needle'. That peaceful view of bookstalls had soon to be modified. They quickly developed into sales points of an importance which serious and committed operators like Menzies and W. H. Smith had scarcely envisaged. With their endless passing trade and swift turnover they became unique little emporia, leading the public taste in reading habits and consumer goods.

Before John Menzies's time very little reading material was produced in a convenient form for the traveller. The Shilling Railway Library of 1846 had been a tentative step in that direction, but a premature one. Genuine railway literature came in with Mrs Gaskell's *Cranford*, first of the famous 'yellowbacks', in 1857, John Menzies's inaugural bookstall year. He sold 'yellowbacks' and tourist guides, which always did well in Scotland, and he gradually allowed his managers to make their own choices from his whole-sale catalogue–choices which reflected idiosyncratic and often inexplicable local demand. Who could say why, as an English bookstalls inspector pointed out,

'religious books hardly find a purchaser at Liverpool, while at the Manchester stations they are in high demand'?

Organised into a junior *corps d'élite*, with uniforms, tallies and identity cards, the basket boys were roving ambassadors for the Menzies firm. The uniform cap is shown here.

Certain managers revelled in this part of their job. There was one at Perth station, known to passengers as the 'literary genius', who attached labels bearing his own recommendations to the novels he offered for sale. (One purchaser, throwing the volume out of the window as the train approached Edinburgh, was heard to mutter that "the chiel who wrote the advert should hae written the book".)

A good selection of daily papers and up-to-date periodicals was every manager's concern and pride. The great advantage of a railway bookstall was that it usually stood within throwing distance of the trains. It had first pick of the London papers. Unofficially, the manager also had access to the station's telegraphic facilities. If the manager at Craigendoran passed word to the manager at Crianlarich that a customer was asking for the *Oban Times*, the *Oban Times* could be on board the next train.

Local newsagents often replenished their own supplies from the station bookstall. Far from rebuffing them, a manager worth his salt would cooperate and send a boy round from time to time to see if anything was wanted, for it looked as though that newsagent's wholesaler was not very efficient and there might be a chance of winning him over to John Menzies.

In the founder's time newspapers didn't circulate all that freely, but there was a large trade in cheap monthlies. In his first bookstall year, 1857, Menzies published advertisements showing how a whole working-class family, provided one member of it was literate, could read or be read to all the year round for the modest outlay of 4/6 (23p); or for half as much, if it went shares with the family next door. He gave an example:

'*British Workman*, 1d
British Messenger, 1½d
Gospel Trumpet, ½d
Children's Paper, 1d
Sabbath School Messenger, ½d'

–five monthly magazines for 4½d (less than 2p) and all, of course, delivered free from your neighbourhood station bookstall.

Numerous sophisticated adjuncts to travel began to appear among the literature at the bookstall; items you couldn't buy anywhere else. You could get a stone hot-water bottle in winter and a patent clip for your straw hat in summer. You could buy a travelling cap, the sort of thing Sherlock Holmes used to be portrayed in, with flaps buttoning under the chin. There were muzzles for dogs, as required by railway regulations. There were candles in holders with rubber vacuum discs for attaching to the seat behind your head–a necessary aid to nervous females and people who wanted to read at night in times when second- and third-class carriages were unlit.

The old-time lumps of black bun, the bottles of beer and the jars of paregoric and stickjaw had vanished; and nothing eatable or drinkable replaced them. The all-powerful refreshment-room proprietors wouldn't allow it.

John Menzies came to bookstalls comparatively late in life, but before he died he must have been assured that *they* had come to stay. They were the place every traveller made for if he had time to wait for his train. Victorian travellers got into the habit of *making* time. They gave themselves an extra ten minutes for a browse at the bookstall, to cast their eyes over the latest titles and the latest novelties, to equip themselves with the necessities (which had once been the luxuries) of the voyage.

4

'Prompt despatch is the secret'

'Prompt despatch is the secret'

'Cash received in business,' as John Menzies's little red memorandum book continued to call it, amounted in 1857 to more than £22,000, a substantial increase on previous years. That was the year of the first bookstall ventures, but not a full one and bookstall receipts accounted for less than five per cent of the sum.

Over the next decade the bookstall receipts represented a respectable percentage of the annual totals. In 1860 they brought in £3,572 out of £27,416. After that the percentage dropped because, while total turnover went up–steadily, not by leaps and bounds–the bookstall receipts remained for a long time at something under £4,000 a year. It was not

a lot, considering the headaches they produced. But the bookstalls were strategical outposts on John Menzies's plan of campaign. In due course those small dots would be joined up to make a picture of a distribution network.

Characteristically the founder anticipated the needs of a new class of tycoon: the newspaper proprietor. Immediate results of the abolition of advertisement duty (1853) and stamp duty (1855) on newspapers were the launchings of two cheap dailies, the *Daily Mail* and *Daily Express*. Handling newsprint in bulk presented problems. The proprietors needed agents in various centres round the British Isles, as the book and magazine proprietors had done. It saved time and money when the national dailies, instead of being made up in individual wrappers for subscribers or into packages for retailers, could be despatched in bales to distributing centres in places like Birmingham, Manchester and Edinburgh, there to be split into smaller parcels and sent out to retailers. It helped the retailer too. He no longer had the bother of separate accounts with the distant head offices of many newspapers. He could have one account for all of them, and that allowed him to adjust and alter his orders more quickly and to cope with the rapidly growing demand.

As the halfpenny newspaper became more and more a part of ordinary people's lives, so the systems devised as conveniences for both ends of the trade became more and more necessities.

John Menzies lost no time in opening accounts with the *Daily Mail* and *Daily Express* and handling their distribution in eastern Scotland from his Edinburgh office. The two papers soon ceased publication (they had no connection with their present-day namesakes) but they'd been straws in

Princes Street, Edinburgh from its junction with Hanover Street. By the middle of the nineteenth century the buildings along the north side of the street had begun to assume their present-day shape. In this picture John Menzies's premises, removed from the small shop round the corner, are shown. Below, the brass plate of Number 12 Hanover Street.

the wind of change. For him they opened up visions of a nationwide distribution agency. What he sowed in his lifetime the firm reaped after his death. The harvest ripened in 1896, when the first mass-circulation dailies began to appear: a new *Daily Mail,* a new *Daily Express,* a *Daily Graphic* (afterwards the *Daily Sketch*) and a *Daily Mirror.*

The Education Acts of 1872 made schooling compulsory in Britain. The first products of the new learning were now adult readers. The daily papers offered them a layout and display of news, with bold typefaces and bright pictures, which put the old 'quality' journals to shame. And they could be had for a fraction of the cost. With offers of free gifts, free insurance and prize crossword competitions, circulation managers drove the figures towards a million copies a day. The term 'press baron' entered the language.

All of that came after the founder's time, but he foresaw it and dropped retail bookselling entirely in order to concentrate on wholesale distribution; lifting his organisation, one might say, across the divide between 'trade' and 'business'. He saw that warehouse and office space beyond the plain bookseller's dreams would be needed, and he moved his firm round the corner from Princes Street to number 2, and later number 12, Hanover Street. It was still equidistant from the two main railway stations of Edinburgh. (The firm moved several times into larger premises as the years went by but never far from Hanover Street. The address 'Hanover Buildings' moved with it. In 1930 Hanover Buildings occupied numbers 66–84 Rose Street, where its corner turret was a feature of Edinburgh's civic-baronial architecture. The turret disappeared in 1978, when the whole place was refurbished, the former warehouse transformed into administrative offices and the exterior given a more up-to-date look.)

John Menzies had five children. In 1867, when he decided to form himself into a company, the two boys, John and Charles, were too young to be a part of it. The founder at that point established a tradition which his heirs have honoured to the present day. He selected four men from the business, Messrs Turner, Macnab, Innes and Mackenzie, and took them into partnership. (We have already met Duncan Macnab: he was Menzies's first employee, hired in 1837.) In a short history of the Menzies group, compiled almost a hundred years later, H.M. Graham notes:

'Prompt despatch is the secret'

'This was a wise innovation, and one the Menzies family have followed.... Every employee in the Group is eligible for election to the Board of Directors. No fewer than eleven of the present directors of the companies that form the Group started as boys and worked their way by stages to the boardroom.'

John Menzies celebrated the establishment of his company by opening his first branch. He took an upstairs room in a building in Royal Bank Square, Glasgow, and turned it into a warehouse with a staff of one manager and two assistants. One of the Menzies relics is a stout leather brief-case with three brass locks and a reversible plate with EDINBURGH on one side and GLASGOW on the other: the inter-departmental mail carrier. There was a Glasgow bag and an Edinburgh bag and every day they were put on the 1 p.m. train at either end, to be collected by a messenger an hour later at the other. Late in the afternoon the bags made the return journey. They lay all night at the station bookstalls and were picked up and taken to their respective offices next morning by a member of the warehouse staff. The Glasgow manager could therefore transmit orders or requests to his head office in the morning and have a reply on his desk first thing next day, or the same evening if he cared to send to the bookstall for it.

As a museum-piece, the old leather bag is nothing to make a fuss about, but it's a reminder of the innocent improvisations of a bygone age, which those who battle with the telephone – and telex-aided communications of today may sometimes envy.

The 'stout leather brief-case'. For many years this bag, alternately labelled "Edinburgh" and "Glasgow", travelled by train between the Waverley (Edinburgh) and Queen Street (Glasgow) stations, carrying correspondence between head office and branch.

There seem to have been misgivings about the planting of an office in Glasgow. John Menzies was aware that he was seeking custom from a predominantly working-class (which at that date still meant largely illiterate) community. The 'Glasgow experiment', however, was moderately successful from the start and the basis of a great leap forward later on.

More than thirty years were to elapse before the firm opened a second branch, and then they plunged into three widely-spaced towns in quick succession: Dundee, Carlisle, Aberdeen. Distribution requirements naturally conditioned the geography of the operation. Perth came next, in 1913, and Dunfermline and Greenock six and seven years later. When the company reached its centenary in 1933 it was distributing books, magazines and newspapers from thirteen branches and warehouses.

While the Glasgow manager found his feet, the Edinburgh headquarters was becoming a busy and progressive establishment. The trade journals noted its expansion, admiring the swiftness of it. Some referred to John Menzies as the 'northern Simpkin Marshall'–that firm being one of the wholesale giants of the London area. (Simpkin Marshall ceased trading in April 1955. Their book export business, the only corner of their empire left to them, was acquired by Wyman & Sons, who afterwards became part of the Menzies group of companies.)

John Menzies the founder died in 1879, aged seventy-one.

Nearly half a century earlier he had sat alone by candlelight, marking proofs of vignette views and guides to the principal Scottish lochs. Now

The 'Glasgow experiment'. The first branch opened by John Menzies & Co. in Royal Bank Square, Glasgow, 1867.

Mr Robert Dickie, 'universally-respected manager in Glasgow', and afterwards a director of the firm.

the ramifications of his business extended over most of those views and lochs, shopkeepers throughout Scotland depended on the smooth running of the enterprise he had created. It was easy for him, a modern captain of commerce might say. He came along on the crest of Railway Mania and the halfpenny press. The public pegged up its expectations and the means of satisfying those expectations were at hand: his schemes could hardly help coming to fruition. So hindsight shows us.

But the founder didn't have the benefit of hindsight. The future was as murky and uncertain to him as it is to us–perhaps more so, because the Victorian era saw tremendous changes in social habits and modes of life which had remained essentially unchanged since the Middle Ages. In John Menzies's line of business the rewards were substantial for someone who could work diligently, calculate a risk and build a reputation. But every step forward was a step in the dark and the penalties of failure were severe: disgrace, destitution, no second chance. He was not the best equipped by circumstance to take advantage of new methods and new ideas. With his old sense of values, his fetish for paying bills promptly, his horror of being under an obligation to anyone, he laboured with handicaps. He didn't toady, he didn't take up politics to secure a commercial advantage; though some of his competitors found it profitable to do so.

Yes, they were times of opportunity. We can see that now. But in his lifetime not everyone shared John Menzies's optimism. Bankrupt booksellers abounded, economists prophesied disaster. Throughout the Victorian age, the golden years of national expansion and prosperity, Jeremiahs of commerce spoke out, mourning the good old days, seeing nothing but catastrophe ahead . . . just as they do today and just as they did, probably, when Old King Cole was a boy. 'These wretched hard times'– meaning the 1850s or the 1890s or any decade in between–were the constant refrains of booksellers and stationers. When John Menzies offered to relieve one little shopkeeper of his newsagency, the shopkeeper candidly told him it was 'the most harassing, unremunerative and confining job it is possible to find'.

The founder had made friends and kept them. It had been impossible to proceed without making enemies in that jostling free-for-all of the bookstall leases and the newsagents' territories. The railway companies, alive to the improving prestige of the platform stance, applied their pressures and played off one bidder against another. Some incidents in the long-running fight between John Menzies of Edinburgh and Robert Graham of Glasgow give the flavour of a typical struggle between two tough businessmen, each able to hold his own, each determined to get his own way.

Menzies wanted to make ground in the west, Graham was keen to open up in the east. Efforts to reach an accommodation by Robert Dickie, Menzies's universally-respected manager in Glasgow, achieved no result. Conflict broke out in August 1891, when Graham and Menzies's entered the bidding for the bookstalls on Queen Street station, Glasgow, previously held by Thomas Murray. The annual rental was already up to £400, but the railway company warned that it would expect £800 or £900 from then on. Menzies's offered £700 for one year. Robert Graham, a bailie (alderman) of Glasgow, offered for three years at £700, £800 and £900. "He has used a good deal of Town Council lobbying," Dickie told his employers. He'd also enlisted the support of Lord Elgin, a staunch Liberal and a member of the

Glasgow finance committee like himself. The North British Railway Company had said privately that they didn't approve of that kind of thing. Dickie learned that Graham had promised them

'to conduct the business better, as we were too old-fashioned and gave too much prominence to books instead of newspapers'.

Queen Street went to Graham. Menzies's next found they had to agree to a big rent rise at Waverley station in Edinburgh. Hints were dropped that Graham was after those bookstalls too, but he swore that that was only a story put about to raise the bidding:

'I never thought of offering for it, never even dreamed of offering . . . of course, should your people attempt to oppose me here (on the Glasgow & South-western line), as I hear they are doing, I shall know how to meet their opposition.'

The railway companies saw the rivalry between the firms and exploited it. Menzies blamed Graham for his rent increase at Waverley, Graham blamed Menzies for his rent increase at Queen Street. Early in 1892 the quarrel moved into a new arena. It came into the open when Graham issued a circular to all the newsagents on the south side of Glasgow:

'I am informed that Messrs Menzies of Edinburgh have opened a second branch on the south side and are stating as an excuse for opening in opposition to me "that I had taken some bookstalls over their heads". . . the statement is an unmitigated and malicious lie and is characteristic of many of their statements. They were so much annoyed at my success (with Queen Street) that before I entered into possession they threatened to oppose me as a Wholesale Newsagent on the south side if I did not give up my lease to them. . . .'

It looks as though Robert Graham took some legal advice after issuing that statement. It was swiftly withdrawn and another, of milder tone, substituted.

That was only one thread in the colourful pattern of negotiation and acquisition that the news distributors were weaving; a pattern, it seems, knotted with irresponsible tittle-tattle by people whose interest it was to keep the big firms at loggerheads. Mr R. V. Nussey, an elder statesman of the house of Menzies, cannot recall that the firm ever had a branch on the south side of Glasgow.

Branch or no branch, orders from the south-side newsagents of Glasgow and from the north, south, east and west sides of many other places poured in. From the 1890s a few daily and weekly newsagents' lists have come to light and they are a revelation for the quantity and diversity of the reading matter a wholesaler's clients asked for. So many hundreds of small items, at individual costs so minuscule, all requiring separate handling . . . where did the profit lie? This random order, for one customer at one tiny corner newsagent's on that notorious south side of Glasgow, has to be multiplied many times for many other customers before we can see what it was the wholesalers were fighting about:

'*Comic Cuts*, ½d; *Chips*, ½d; *Chatterbox*, ½d; *Boy's Friend*, ½d; *Daily Record* ½d; *Glasgow Evening News*, ½d; *Glasgow Herald*, 1d; *Scotsman*, 1d; *Daily Mail*, 1d; *Punch*, 3d.'

That was a total of ten items, gathered in by the Menzies organisation from London, Glasgow, Edinburgh and Dundee, sorted and sent out again and placed on the doorsteps of ten terraced houses at Bridgeton Cross; and

Bailie (afterwards Sir) Robert Graham of Glasgow, prominent in wholesale news distribution and local politics in the west of Scotland for more than sixty years.

all for ninepence (less than 4p). Such orders were fulfilled morning and evening, daily, weekly and monthly, through little shops by the thousand and larger shops by the hundred, every item funnelled through the wholesaler's warehouse and dealt with at speed, while the cities slept.

The nation's definitions of 'news' and 'topicality' were being revised year by year. It was no longer enough to have a sight of a daily paper three or four days after it was published: the 1890s householder wanted it on the mat at breakfast-time. The system demanded special skills and contingency planning of some quality. That was where Menzies's scored over their rivals. Reporting the firm's arrival in Aberdeen in 1898 with 'a great wholesale newsagency and distributing office . . . lighted by electricity', the *Northern Chronicle* stated what observers all over Scotland could endorse:

'The business done is enormous. . . . Prompt despatch is the secret of John Menzies & Company's success.'

You could lobby town councils and spread tales about your opponents and construct all manner of webs of intrigue, but in the end you rose or fell by the enduring efficiency of your operation.

Book titles of a bygone era. A few examples of the hundreds of books, magazines and novels in weekly parts which were familiar sights on station bookstalls and made available through the Menzies service to countless readers at their homes.

5

'The whole tempo changed'

'The whole tempo changed'

John R. Menzies, eldest son of the founder, head of the firm for forty-eight years. (See *The Menzies Dynasty*, page 94.)

In an old family business, especially one which believes in promotion on merit, employees tend to start young and stay all their lives. The arches of the years stretch onward, but old-timers' reminiscences compress them into short span: "I mind his grandfather well."

Company staff now approaching retirement age may still have personal memories of the present chairman's grandfather and great-uncle, the two sons of John Menzies who took control of the company when the founder died. John Ross Menzies ('John R.') resigned as chairman in 1932 and died three years later. His brother Charles Thompson Menzies ('Charles T.') was chairman after him until *his* death in 1943.

The two boys–they were not much more than boys in 1879–showed themselves true sons, thoroughly indoctrinated in the founder's principles of thrift and devotion to duty; to which they added a capacity for unremitting toil at which old John Menzies himself might have stood amazed. They began, says H. M. Graham,

'to work like beavers. They knew what had to be done and, quite simply, did it. Office hours meant nothing to them and their enthusiasm at times caused their executives nightmares. Peter Nisbet . . . used to recall in after years how, as a boy, he was sent to the brothers' house in Grosvenor Crescent [Edinburgh] for the lunchtime snacks. Back at the office John or Charles would clear a space on the desk, motion the sandwiches to be laid down and with the minimum of distraction would return to the job in hand. Their industry was phenomenal, but it paid dividends.'

Of John R., the senior, Mr Graham says:

'The whole tempo of the firm's life changed under his management.'

Horizons widened. By the end of the century the firm could consider itself a national concern, with a news department serving all Scotland, a group of bookstalls which covered most railway stations and a solid connection with the main-street booksellers and stationers of the principal Scottish towns. In 1891, before such things as H.M. Stationery Offices were thought of, John Menzies & Company acquired the agency for the sale of all Government publications in Scotland for a period of ten years.

Bailie, a once-renowned west-of-Scotland weekly, reported in October 1910 the snapping of a link with the distant past:

'The great house of Menzies, wholesale booksellers and publishers of Edinburgh and Glasgow, was built up under John Menzies the first, along with Messrs Turner, Macnab, Innes and Mackenzie, all of whom were eventually assumed as partners. The old order changes, for the last of the band, Mr Gershom Steel Mackenzie, died a week ago. Mr John and Mr Charles Menzies, sons of the founder, are now the heads of the firm. Menzies & Co., which has a goldmine in the bookstall business, crept up gradually until it is the largest concern of its kind in Scotland.'

Those four young men had been the first of the executives drawn from the lower strata of the business. In June 1906, when the partners decided to register under the Companies Act and become John Menzies & Company Limited, they appointed as co-directors the manager of their Edinburgh warehouse, Mr William Dawson, and the manager of their Glasgow branch, Mr Robert Dickie. Seventy years later you would find in the boardroom others who, like them, had started at the most modest levels: a former assistant from the Carlisle news department, a former apprentice in the Edinburgh book department, a former boy from the Dundee stockroom, a former boy from the Glasgow book saloon. They were living testimonies of a philosophy encapsulated in the chairman's remark: "I never promote a man. The man promotes himself."

A few employees responded to the call which Scottish lads through the ages have found hard to resist: the call to emigrate. John Sherriff, on the founder's recommendation, went to Australia and set up a chain of book-shops and in due course Menzies's established an export agency with him. During Edwardian times another Menzies-trained man, Thomas Hislop, gave up his job as manager of the Perth bookstall to become inspector of all the railway bookstalls in New South Wales. In 1910, when South African Railways wanted someone to organise a station-bookstall network on the Menzies pattern, they hired a Menzies inspector to take charge.

Case histories of Menzies employees on the whole, however, suggest that if you survived the first year or two you were there for life. From pre-First World War days the picture comes down to us of a hierarchical but by no means feudal concern, not so large that the directors couldn't hope to know every member of the staff; a business which functioned as one large, somewhat far-flung family. If the amount of leisure activity corporately indulged in is any guide to an organisation's health, John Menzies & Company was healthy.

In newspaper reports and the faded décor of concert programmes and menus we have vivid portrayals of staff get-togethers on summer after-noons and winter evenings, outdoors and in, of an epoch when people cultivated their own resources and knew how to amuse themselves; when a group of a dozen or so included at least one pianist, one or more singers and the rest capable of a comic recitation–taken, probably, from some Menzies publication such as *Readings Pithy and Pawky, Humorous Readings Maistly Scotch* or *Dialogues Unco' Funny.* Elderly Scots at home and abroad still write to the firm to ask if those collections of verses and anecdotes ('Pithy! Pawky! Piquant!–Cheerful! Choice! Charming!') are still available. Who knows what happy oc-casions of long ago their memories are tied to?

Menzies's in Edinburgh had its Social and Sports Club. In Glasgow, just to be different, they had a Sports and Social Club. As staff increased, so the proposals for clubs proliferated and some went farther than mere proposals. Bowls and Putting clubs, Tennis and Swimming clubs, Skittles and Badminton clubs . . . for a time there was even a John Menzies Madrigal Choir. Country dance classes were a great hit. Dancing was a positive addiction of the Carlisle branch staff, we're told. Their manager was a bowls fanatic. In his absence on Saturday afternoons the assist-ants closed the doors, posted lookouts and practised their steps.

The firm's football team (Hanover Thistle, light green jerseys, dark green hoops) played in one of the Lothians leagues. For many years the ladies' hockey team was a highly competitive outfit in central Scotland. Later came basketball, with a place in the Edinburgh & District league. (The latest from Edinburgh in 1981 was a Ski club and mixed male-and-female hockey and football teams.)

Charles T. Menzies, second son of the founder, here portrayed as Master of the Berwickshire Hunt. (See *The Menzies Dynasty*, page 94.)

Centre:
Stalwarts of the John Menzies
Rambling Club, drawn from
members of the headquarters and
Edinburgh station bookstall staffs,
dressed up to have their photo-
graphs taken in Princes Street
Gardens, Edinburgh, in 1884.

The firm took delivery of its first
motor-van, an Argyll, in 1910. This
vehicle, price £383.17.8 ex works,
was the prototype of a large fleet.

As long ago as 1886 the Rambling club was formed—when the word 'rambling' was hardly known. Its first outing was to Craigmillar Castle on the outskirts of Edinburgh. These days, notices of coming events and reports of dances, summer outings, excursions and Christmas parties at headquarters and branches all over the country fill two or three pages of the house magazine.

Country staff had no reason to regret being remote from the action. Up to and beyond Edwardian days, when the station bookstall was part of the daily scene of every traveller, the Menzies assistants were often minor celebrities with large circles of friends; and Menzies managers, like the local doctors or ministers, were pillars of their communities. If they changed jobs, the fact was noticed in the press. Mr James Baird, on completing a seven-year stint as manager of the Menzies bookstall in Aberdeen,

'was met by a large number of railway officials and others in one of the waiting rooms last night and presented with a handsome piano'.

A piece of plate, suitably inscribed, was also presented to Mr Baird. The

company heard songs from Messrs Anderson, Dinnie and Rae of the railway company and Miss Howie put the piano through its paces and accompanied the final chorus of *Auld Lang Syne*. The local newspaper summarised the numerous votes of thanks and added one of its own to

'a tactful, obliging and courteous manager, one who did not spare him-self . . . (whose) promotion was well deserved. Messrs Menzies had not got a more conscientious servant . . .'.

In the Highland fastnesses the social life of John Menzies's employees was sometimes conducted at an impressive level. The manageress at Ballater bookstall, terminus of the Deeside line, always had an invitation to the ghillies' ball at Balmoral, where the royal family danced with the servants and estate workers. For a hundred years that bookstall served the Castle during the royal holiday month, until the station closed down in 1961. The manageress explained the routine:

'The sergeant footman orders the papers. Morning papers are collected by a soldier from the royal guard of honour, and the London dailies by one of the chauffeurs. . . . Royalty on leaving generally visit the bookstall to choose papers for the homeward journey.'

The manageress learned to keep likely commodities in stock, there being little in the way of stationery or fancy goods in the neighbourhood. But little Prince Michael of Kent stumped her with a request for a seaside pail and she had to make a dash to Aberdeen for one.

Her colleague at Bonar Bridge, farther north, received a piece of wedding cake from the Duke and Duchess of Kent in recognition of services rendered–women's magazines, chiefly–to the bride when she was Miss Worsley.

A bookstall staff was a microcosm of the Menzies organisation, a replica in miniature of the family-style headquarters nucleus. The manager took quite a fatherly interest in the welfare of his little flock. Mr Harry Light, a bookstall superintendent, harking back to boyhood days around 1906, recalled how the manager taught his boys boxing and how, at seven of a Sunday morning, he would knock at their doors to take them for a long walk. Some might have considered that going a little too far; on the other hand, for those who had to present themselves at the bookstall at 5.30 a.m. six days a week, the lie-in until seven may have been a luxury.

Readings Pithy and Pawky, one of a series of Menzies publications which contained anecdotes, funny tales, dialogues and poems suitable for recitation–an indispensable purchase for anyone on his way to a soiree or dinner where he might be called on to make a speech or do a "turn".

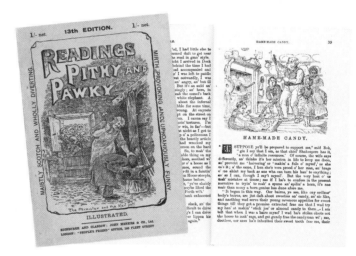

Years on, from veterans like Harry Light who converged as some social evening progressed and formed a little club of their own in a corner, newcomers gained insight into the lore and legend of the company and its everyday life in days gone by. To hear them talk you would imagine that fifty years had passed in the twinkling of an eye, that railways and newspapers had been invented the week before last and that they themselves had known the dubious delights of stage-coach travel in wintertime.

Mr Light, who started with Wyman's and afterwards became a Menzies employee, harked back to the turn of the century when 'nothing in the matter of possible business was neglected'. Between trains, he and the other boys were sent out on foot or hired bicycles to build up a round–to carry samples of books and magazines in their baskets and try and interest local people in them.

Robert Dickie was long acknowledged the grand old man of the veterans' corner. He was heavily-built, with a noble head and a spade beard. He had been Menzies's first Glasgow manager and the first director to bear a name other than Menzies. Having been entrusted with many delicate negotiations in his fifty-two years with the firm he could reminisce about Robert Graham the bailie and 'Diary' Murray and the tug-o'-wars with them; and about skirmishes with railway companies, licensing authorities and assessors about the perpetually vexed questions of tobacconists' early-closing days and the rateable values of platform stances.

William James Rhind, another director, looked back not quite so far. He had taken out articles with Menzies's in 1876 as an apprentice bookseller. He recalled that in his young days a newsagent with a 'list' worth £5 a week was a newsagent of substance. As to books, the greatest best-seller he had handled was J. J. Bell's *Wee Macgreegor,* price one shilling (5p).

Scarcely qualified to join in when the Edwardian stalwarts talked their life histories was James Leckie, then in his middle thirties. He was a well-known figure in Scottish journalistic and sporting circles. His eventual working span of fifty-four years was not exceptional for Menzies's, though it would have been for many companies. He had begun as a message boy at the Glasgow branch in 1883. He remembered the abuse he got from customers, as though the increase in the price of certain daily papers, from a halfpenny to a penny, was all his fault. Evening papers remained at a halfpenny. Sunday papers in Scotland didn't exist.

Leckie's first job was delivering parcels of newspapers to the various retailers. He toured Glasgow by horse-tram and steam-tram, throwing the packages to the waiting newsagents at each corner. In those days everyone read *Bailie, Chiel* and *Quiz*–everyone in the west of Scotland, at any rate. The old football journals, *Scottish Athletic, Scottish Sport* and *Scottish Referee,* also had huge circulations. Leckie had a part-time job on the last-named. In his later years he became a director of Partick Thistle F.C. and a Scottish selector. Around the firm he was pointed out as the man who first recognised the genius of a teenaged Raith Rovers forward named Alex James, whom Arsenal bought for an unprecedented £9000 and who made one of a memorable Scottish forward line in the late 1920s.

A historic day for the firm, Mr Leckie recalled, was the day in 1910 when it took delivery of its first motor-van, an Argyll of the antiquated covered-wagon type. Solid tyres. Price £383.17.8. Up to then John R. Menzies's stables had supplied the motive power for the delivery vans. Ten years later the firm was running a few war-surplus ambulances and beginning to replace them with Morris Commercial vans. A white-faced chestnut horse was still in action in 1920.

When the veterans of the firm got on to finance, they would remember that the business returned profits at a steady rate throughout the 1880s and 1890s, fluctuating around £8000 a year; and that in 1906, when Menzies's became a limited company, profits shot up to £15,000 a year and showed a continuing upward trend for some years after that.

Regarding wages past and present (a subject to which a conclave of veterans inevitably returns in the end), their own cases would illustrate how senior executives of the future are marked out and pushed forward at an early stage in their careers. Wage-sheets of the 1880s generally identify the newcomers of promise, those who will be near the top in thirty or forty years' time.

James Leckie is typical. Just turned eleven, he starts in 1883 at £12 a year. By 1890 he is earning £50 a year, a fast rise to an exceptionally good wage for an eighteen-year-old. Advancement to assistant brings him into the £70-£90-a-year bracket. And before the century is out he is earning £220 a year as manager of the Glasgow branch.

A much more important personality–to young members of the firm, at least–than chairman or managing director was James Leckie, a veteran who retired in 1937. He had worked his way up from message boy to director but his prestige rested on his part-time activities: sporting journalist, football club director and Scottish international selector.

6

'The arrangement is a splendid one'

'The arrangement is a splendid one'

Appointment to the bookstall on Carlisle station, one of the busiest bookstalls in the British Isles and Menzies's largest south of the Border for many years, set the seal on many a manager's career. This picture postcard with its turbulent news placards dates from 1915.

Wyman & Sons' delivery vans were familiar sights in the traffic of London, the Midlands and the West of England after that firm's swift takeover of three hundred and fifty bookstalls in 1906.

Edinburgh, 1908. Year of the International Exhibition in Saughton Park and an influx of visitors, most of whom saw their first aeroplane there.

John Menzies's, 1908. The midpoint of its history to date, seventy-five years from the reflective, discursive, easy-paced little world of the bookshop on Princes Street, seventy-five years from the present day, when the affairs of John Menzies are the affairs of hundreds of branches and shops and millions of shoppers.

These first few years of the twentieth century are the halcyon days of the story magazine, the boys' and girls' papers, the family weeklies and the heavy monthlies; and some newspapers have reached daily circulations of a million copies. To cope with them Menzies's have warehouses and distributing centres in the four main Scottish cities and at Carlisle across the Border.

In 1908 the name of Menzies comes chiefly before the public eye on the front of a railway bookstall, though bookstalls never were and never will be the most important element in the company's fortunes. By this date the big five have emerged, the five bookstall princes who have carved up the railway routes and apportioned the stations out between them and, despite recent shocks, appear to have stabilised the position and to be preserving a watchful neutrality towards each other. The big five are:

W. H. Smith & Son Ltd, biggest of the bookstall networks, controlling about five hundred sites in England.

John Menzies & Company Ltd, holding most Scottish stations and the Carlisle area.

Robert Graham & Company, who rent the Glasgow & South-western Railway bookstalls. (We met him in Chapter 4: he lived to serve more than seventy years in the trade, and to be knighted. Only death loosened his grip on the Clyde coast stances and Menzies's didn't acquire them until 1933.)

Wyman & Sons, a firm hardly anyone outside the trade had heard of until 1906 when, in a brilliantly-timed and neatly-executed operation, they opened three hundred and fifty English bookstalls, taking over many L.&N.W.R. and G.W.R. leases from W. H. Smith & Son, including Euston, Paddington and Temple Meads, Bristol.

Entwined with the history and development of railway stations and platform amenities throughout England, the bookstalls of W. H. Smith & Son flourished unchallenged for nearly sixty years. This illustration shows a typical Smith's layout during the first quarter of the present century.

Messrs Eason of Dublin, with eighty-eight bookstalls in Ireland.

Eason's, the Irish counterpart of John Menzies of Scotland, are worth a mention in any survey of bookstall pioneers. The firm's founder, Charles Eason, had been W. H. Smith's bookstall manager in Manchester. They sent him to Dublin to open a bookshop in 1856. The premises had no space for a window display, but Charles Eason attracted custom by posting sporting results at the door–the Boat Race, Derby, St Leger and so on–telegraphed from England. On behalf of Smith's he took over numerous bankrupt booksellers in different parts of Ireland and in 1868 he opened a branch in Belfast.

Mr W. H. Smith, the head of the parent company, was a cabinet minister and in 1886 was appointed Secretary of State for Ireland. Judging it improper to have business interests there, he transferred everything ("on most generous terms," said Eason's son) to his manager in Dublin; a decision he must have instantly regretted, for the Government fell within days and his secretaryship with it. But Smith stuck to his bargain.

Eason and his son developed bookshops and newsagents all over the island. They maintained the sporting interest: their commemorative picture postcards after the Gordon Bennett Cup races and the first aerial crossing of the Irish Sea are now much sought after. About 1900 a traveller in Ireland reported that at Eason's in Sackville Street (now O'Connell Street) you could buy gramophone records, shampoo, bay rum and setting lotions, permanent wave sachets, electrical goods, razors and shaving brushes, hairpins, nail clippers and electric eyebrow tweezers–extraordinary novelties for pre-Edwardian Ireland.

When Eire became a political reality, business fell off. Continental competition increased, expanding bus services ruined the railway trade and the firm sold stocks at a heavy loss. But Eason's faced recession boldly, opening branches in Derry and Limerick and taking over a big wholesaler at Waterford. They spent their way out of trouble and they flourish in the 1980s, along with two (Smith's and Menzies's) of the original big five.

Midway through our history, all five are doing well. The iron horse marches on. (In Scotland in 1908 light railways are all the rage. They boast sleeping cars–to the back door of the Turnberry Hotel in Ayrshire, from the London-Stranraer express; cow-catchers–on the Fraserburgh–St Combs line; Britain's westernmost station–Machrihanish in Argyll; the highest station in the British Isles–Wanlockhead in Dumfriesshire, 1498 feet; and there are plans for building more, all over the Highlands and on Lewis and Skye.)

Bookstalls mark every interstice in the web. Pride and prestige must keep many of them going. Superficially they seem to bring their managers nothing but toil and trouble. Menzies's man at Montrose works a twelve-hour day. It is longer in summer, because his station receives excursion trains, the first coming in at five a.m. and the last one leaving at 11 p.m. and it is his duty to serve them. In winter, as on most Scottish lines, fog, snow and ice cause delays but, as the manager says,

'it is unthinkable that the bookstall should close before the last train departs'.

At Turriff in Aberdeenshire, by an old tradition the coldest place in Scotland, the manager writes feelingly of having to sweep away snow before he can open the bookstall door and of having to break the ice in the ink-bottle before he can start making up his accounts.

Almost by definition the bookstall is a draughty box, sited at the most windswept spot on the platform. Under milder western skies the problems, as the Irvine, Ayrshire, manageress points out, are that

'on sunny days we have to cover up the chocolate to keep it from melting, on wet days the rain comes in and soaks the newspapers. On windy days the posters are in tatters five minutes after we put them out and the wee stall rocks on its foundations.'

A manager's newsboys are a constant anxiety. They are too nimble for their own safety. In 1907, the basket boy Joseph M'Carron died in the Elliot Junction (Arbroath) derailment. Three years before that, at Glasgow Central station, a train crashed through the buffers and the locomotive ended up in the middle of the bookstall.

Bookstall managers on rural stations receive a weekly wage of 27/- (£1.35) and are considered not ill-paid. School-leavers aged thirteen, employed full-time, may earn five shillings (25p) for a week of up to a hundred and eight hours. In the bustle of arrivals and departures at a busy station like Edinburgh Waverley, with the newspapers sailing into the carriage windows and the money for them sailing out, it's not unknown for the basket boy to catch half-a-crown (12½p) thrown in mistake for a penny. Of course, the train has gone before he notices it.

By 1908 the poor law inspectors, burgh assessors and county assessors have given up levying rates on John Menzies's bookstalls. A painful war of attrition which satisfied only the lawyers has ended. Station bookstalls in England and Scotland will remain free of local rates and Schedule 'A' income-tax until 1936. The manageress at Irvine mentioned chocolate: by arrangement with the refreshment-room proprietors, some bookstalls can now sell sweets and fruits.

The thorny question of early-closing hours will not be resolved until 1919. Bookstalls should be exempted from the Acts because they have to open at all sorts of odd times and the assistants arrange time off among themselves. Menzies's accept a prosecution for infringement of the Shops Act and take the matter to the high court, where three judges allow their

A poke of sweets for the journey. After many years of wrangling with station refreshment-room proprietors the bookstall operators secured the right to stock fresh fruit and jars of boiled sweets.

appeal. It's decided that they needn't observe tobacconists' hours either, because tobacco sales are only part of their business. But the prohibition on selling smokers' requisites after eight p.m. is held to apply.

So the station bookstalls appear to be winning all along the line, and the successes of the big firms which run them are arousing envy in small traders. The *Stationery Trade Review*:

'It has been a grievance of long standing with publishers . . . that a monopoly of nine-tenths of all the railway bookstalls in the country should be in the hands of two firms, one in England, Messrs W. H. Smith & Son, and the other in Scotland, Messrs John Menzies & Co. Local booksellers and newsagents have winced and fretted under a system they were powerless to alter; and in the long run most of them have acquiesced in it so far that for years they have been getting their books and newspapers through the same firms. No wonder the two businesses have grown to gigantic proportions . . . the arrangement is a splendid one for them.'

John Menzies & Co., the writer goes on, have all their parcels delivered free. Their employees have to sign an agreement not to make an offer for a stall on the expiry of a lease, even after they themselves have left the firm. In short, Menzies's have an unfair advantage and are taking the bread out of shopkeepers' mouths–and not only the mouths of booksellers and newsagents:

'Besides supplying books and newspapers, this firm also does an extensive trade in tobaccoes, cutlery, playing cards, travelling rugs and souvenir knick-knacks . . . and also takes orders for printing, binding and picture-framing.'

A publisher named Maxwell, who is also a Great Western Railway shareholder, proposes at an annual general meeting that the railways shall redistribute the bookstalls to break 'this injurious monopoly'; but finds no support. (In England, Wyman's broke it for him.) Another trade paper, *The Stationer*, takes up the cause protesting

'against our large railway companies permitting general stores to be opened and conducted on their premises. . . . The railway station is a very attractive place to make a display of goods, there are no rates and taxes to pay, the holders of the stall contribute nothing to the town. . . . It is utterly unfair to allow bookstalls at railway stations to sell anything but news-papers and books.'

Menzies's might have argued that the undeniable attractions of the sites were taken into account when the railway companies fixed their exorbitant rents; and that the bookstalls came up for letting every five years and anyone could bid for them.

In 1908 there's an occasional echo of 'something biting about bookstalls' in the public press: a letter about assistants who know only two phrases, "Haven't got it" and "Don't stock it"; a complaint about the jostling crowds at the counter, 'every one of them being no doubt strong supporters of the Old Age Pensions scheme, and feeding and clothing their children at the expense of the State'. But dissatisfied customers are neither so numerous nor so vociferous as they were, and for each one who complains, two rush to the concessionaire's defence. The *Glasgow Evening News*:

'To attack the contents and methods of the railway bookstall has become the stock device of the writer hard up for a literary topic. . . *The Nation* last month had an article on the bookstalls of France, with which the Scottish

Playing cards were among the items sold on station bookstalls which, said the trade papers on behalf of small local stationers, made for "utterly unfair" competition against honest shop-keepers in small communities.

were unfavourably compared. Last week there was another piece extolling the bookstalls of Spain over both the French and the British . . . probably it will soon be discovered that the railway bookstalls of Finland are still better, while we may reasonably expect someone to put in a word on behalf of Russia. . . .'

The *Aberdeen Journal* (this is still 1908) pays a tribute to the stylish Menzies bookstalls at Banchory and Ballater on the royal route of Deeside. When Menzies's, having taken over all the old Highland Railway bookstalls, replaces the archaic wreck at Inverness station with a stall of the most modern type, the *Inverness Courier* advises its readers to go and see this

'very roomy and ornate stall . . . (which) presents a very pretty kiosque-like appearance . . . varnished and finished in the most tasteful manner.'

Thomas Maclaren, outgoing tenant at Inverness, tells a reporter that he is handing over a list of not less than a hundred publications. When he first went to Inverness in 1863 there wasn't a single newspaper on sale.

The *Glasgow Herald* is so generous with its compliments that you would think the bookstall manager himself wrote them:

'Since the bookstall at the Central station came under Messrs Menzies's management there have been decided improvements both in its appearance and the attention paid to passengers, who can now depend on an endless assortment of suitable literature for railway travelling. The boon is much appreciated by the public, and Messrs John Menzies & Co. have to be congratulated on their enterprise.'

Taking a consensus around 1908, the efficiency of the station bookstall staff is confirmed almost by acclamation. Nor are tributes lacking to more personal qualities. A letter to the *Perth Advertiser:*

'If Burns had lived in the land of Scotland today he would assuredly have written many a charming verse to "The Lass that Sold my Poems to Me" at Bonnie Dundee or Bridge of Allan or some other of the Messrs Menzies's bookstalls in the North, presided over by Scotia's fair daughters.'

The Menzies bookstall on Glasgow Central station. Down the years this great splash of colour in the middle of the concourse has been not only a place for Scots heading south to do their last-minute shopping but also a point of rendezvous as famous in Scotland as "under the clock on Victoria station" has been in England.

7

'Porridge and the Shorter Catechism'

'Porridge and the Shorter Catechism'

When war broke out in 1914, the two Menzies brothers had been at the head of the firm for thirty-five years. Of their temperaments, their personal interests and circles of human relationships not much has been recorded (but we know that Charles was a friend of H.M. Stanley, the African explorer). By all accounts they kept themselves too busy to have much of a private life.

Charles, the younger, married into the Aitken family, well-known as the leading brewers in Falkirk until Bass Charrington took them over. He inclined, as far as possible, to the life of the country gentleman, resided in Berwickshire and held a commission in the county yeomanry. Within the firm he was usually known as Colonel Charles. He and his wife were keen on hunting. In 1916, the year he went to Flanders, he was profiled, with a frontispiece portrait, in the riding journal *Baily's Magazine*.

John R., the elder, remained a bachelor all his life. He was the guiding spirit of Menzies's for more than half a century. His shrewdness and ambition kept the business thriving, beating off competition and advancing sure-footed towards a great future. He may be said to have un-locked the door which opened up the firm's formidable wholesaling potential.

An obituarist described him as one who shunned busi-ness contacts and avoided the limelight; certainly he looks, from his photographs, a rather introverted, forbidding person. One suspects that those craggy features and severe expression hid a large and liberal heart. (One also sus-pected it of his father, and we know it was the case with his nephews.)

When smalltime booksellers, newsagents and stationers were at their wits' ends to know what to do for money, John R. took them under his wing–all in the way of business, no doubt, and with an eye to future goodwill, yet some of their letters of gratitude have the ring of thankfulness to a real benefactor. But an echo of his father's sermonising comes with the warnings that loans are condi-tional on the borrowers 'attending carefully to their business'.

And there was something almost shame-faced about the notes which accompanied John R.'s unsolicited contributions to bereaved widows and dependants of some of his poorer clients, as though it was all wrong for a streak of sentiment to appear in a business relationship.

World War I put everybody under strain. But the unprecedented mobility of the population and the demand for reading matter created opportunities too. A military tribunal, granting temporary exemption to the bookstall manager at Perth station, was told that 'practically all the newspapers for the Fleet' passed through his hands.

The company lost forty-six employees out of the two hundred and seventy-six who left to join the armed forces. A note in a trade paper that 'W.H. Smith & Son sent more than a thousand men to the colours' indi-cates the relative sizes of the two firms at that period. The names of the Menzies employees who never returned were inscribed on two war memorials in Hanover Buildings in Edinburgh.

The directors celebrated Armistice Day, 1918, by presenting all the staff with two weeks' income:

'They shall not grow old. . . .' Names of the Menzies employees who died on active service in two World Wars are inscribed on these memorials at the main entrance of the firm's headquarters in Hanover Buildings, Edinburgh.

'as a thank-offering for the cessation of this dreadful war . . . and in recognition of the generous and whole-hearted service rendered to us.'

Commercially the hard times came later: in the early 1920s, a nightmare era of stagnating markets and industrial unrest. Hardly a meeting of directors and branch managers passed without a reference to 'these troublous years through which the company and the country are passing'. The firm's difficulties are reflected in the annual balance sheets. Directors' fees, for instance, were cut from £3000 a year in 1921 to £1000 a year in 1922.

Men who had grown grey in the service saw no way through the gloom. Sir Robert Graham, that old adversary who had successfully mixed business with politics and so obstinately defended his territory on the south side of Glasgow, appeared at a luncheon which John R. gave to the Scottish newsagents in Edinburgh's Assembly Rooms. He made a speech lamenting the vanished era of wholesale expansion so conclusively that anyone listening must have felt it had gone for ever. He was one who could speak with some authority. He'd seen more of the business than anyone present, perhaps more than any man alive, for his involvement with newspaper distribution went back sixty-three years, almost to the date when the first John Menzies made his daring offer for his first little bookstall. Sir Robert stressed the essential vulnerability of retail newsagents in good times and bad, since

'their stock is different every day, and what they don't sell today is unlikely to be sold tomorrow. They have to be more up-to-date than the greengrocer or the baker.'

Trade journals, hobbies, women's interests, story magazines, politics and religion . . . all were catered for by scores of flimsy periodicals in the early years of the 20th century, distributed through newsagents to every corner of the land.

Despite setbacks and grim forecasts John Menzies & Company pressed ahead, spending money, enlarging their bookstall operations and taking businesses off the hands of owners exhausted in the struggle. Finlay's, the Scottish tobacconists whose kiosks often stood cheek-by-jowl with a station bookstall, succumbed to a Menzies bid in 1922. Two venerable Edinburgh businesses which had been flourishing when the founder rented his shop at 61 Princes Street, the advertising agencies of Keith's and Robertson & Scott, were in trouble. Menzies's took over Keith's and bought the news delivery department of Robertson & Scott.

Up to the 1920s the trend had been towards concentration: wholesale distribution and bookstall operations. During that decade, the era of perturbation for booksellers and newsagents, the Menzies brothers sought to diversify. It was essential to keep up the momentum, to keep the machine rolling.

Over the previous fifty years the only book which had appeared under the John Menzies imprint was a little monograph on the schooling of ponies, by the Marchioness of Breadalbane. Publishing had brought the firm some esteem, but little profit; but now they toyed with publishing again. The lists of the 1920s are not very exciting. They contain collections of comic tales and party dialogues of the *Humorous Readings Maistly Scotch* variety; and a few guide-books and publicity brochures, the sort of illustrated booklets which the prospective holidaymaker might obtain by writing to the Town Clerk and enclosing a sixpenny postal order. It all

Prominent among the cheap paperbacks sold in thousands at railway bookstalls were the spy thrillers of E. Phillips Oppenheim and the crime novels of Edgar Wallace. To meet the travelling public's insatiable demands, Edgar Wallace once wrote a complete novel between Friday night and Monday morning.

helped to utilise the warehouse space and keep the employees on the pay-roll.

Reading was a luxury the British public never denied itself, even in the most depressing times. In its warehouses, the firm handled, and at the bookstalls it displayed, a broad range of cheap books and periodicals–cheap by the standards of the times, rather more costly than before. By 1914 the sixpenny illustrated magazine had killed off the penny novelette; the 'yellowback', a longstanding mainstay of the reading masses, had given way to sober classics and modern novels costing up to 6/6 (32p) apiece. (Ian Hay, when a schoolmaster at Fettes, recalled how the Waverley bookstall manager, a critical authority like his Perth colleague before him, would write out his own puffs and stick them on the plain cloth covers of the books, saying 'A tear and a smile on every page' or 'Opens a window into a woman's soul' or something equally fetching.)

After the war the halfpenny comic papers returned. There were weeklies which catered for every phase of childhood, from *Chick's Own* to the *Magnet*. There were sixpenny thrillers and sporting and adventure stories, Edgar Wallace, Sidney Horler, Nat Gould and Zane Grey being the most sought-after authors. There was a superior range at sevenpence (3p) where you might find the works of Jeffrey Farnol, P.G. Wodehouse and E. Phillips Oppenheim.

The wholesaler, no less than the bookseller and the journalist, had to keep abreast of literary affairs. He had to know about the coming names in authorship and to monitor a tremendous outpouring of writers in fact and fiction. It was not his job to mould fashion, but he had to meet fashion's demands and mirror it. The war had been a watershed in fashions, in all aspects of life. Nothing would be quite the same again. Tensions relaxed, old moral precepts tottered, people didn't know exactly where they stood. Literature reflected that too, at all levels. The dealer in the printed word faced new dilemmas.

Or rather, intensifications and sharpenings of old dilemmas. Menzies's had occasionally been under fire in the past for displaying 'vile books'. There'd been the case of Byron's *Don Juan*, then of the 'depraved filth' of Thomas Hardy's *Tess* and *Jude the Obscure*. An attack in the *Pall Mall Gazette* by Grant Allen on the novel *The Woman Who Did* had prompted Smith's, Menzies's and Eason's to recall every copy from their bookstalls.

Menzies's bore the brunt of moral crusades. Menzies's had become the principal distributors of reading matter in Scotland, a country where Victorian prudery died hard. In the conventional Scottish household, fathers still read to their wives and families of an evening, a custom which prescribed in novelists a degree of reticence in the descriptions of romantic love which is hardly credible today. The fictional heroine might be seen for whole chapters on her death-bed, but never on her marriage-bed; and never, never on the bed of shame.

But writers and publishers were always prepared to challenge convention and when something *risqué* slipped through the innocent purchaser (or more often his daughter) could plead that they 'got it at the bookstall'. Scandal erupted. Menzies's name suffered. When a charge was brought (under Acts of 1846, relating to gross indecency), the person who exposed the book for sale had to answer it. Few charges were easier to make, or harder to refute, than of obscenity in the printed word–a term which meant different things to different people, which changed with the moral climate and which, in any case, was virtually undefinable in law.

Just before the First World War the pendulum of taste had swung. British vulgarity asserted itself with the seaside postcard, an item which bookstalls and newsagents in resort towns could hardly be expected *not* to stock. *Civis* of Aberdeen, writing to the *Press & Journal:*

'On some of the railway lines it is impossible for a modest woman to look at the bookstalls without having her sense of modesty outraged by one or other of the dreadful postcards that illustrate flirtations between amorous snobs and girls in bathing costumes.'

About that period, when Edward VII was on the throne, spicy tales of royal misdemeanours enjoyed a vogue among readers of the so-called 'society' papers. The *Dundee Advertiser* noted that one magazine had

'recently published some scandalous allegations regarding persons in high life. Though the charges were made in veiled language, there could be no doubt what they meant. The sale of that particular issue was not only stopped, but the paper has been *permanently banished* from the bookstalls. . . .'

According to *The Leader,* that harsh sentence was the result of 'a request from a high and influential personage to our leading wholesale newsagents'–John Menzies & Co. Ltd. One can't help wondering what it was all about, considering the amount of scurrilous gossip which did get through. It may have been a whisper of what in 1911 was known as the Mylius affair: a rumour that King George V's marriage to Queen Mary was a bigamous one, because years earlier, in Malta, he'd got himself married secretly to Admiral Culme-Seymour's daughter. The King was obliged to bring a libel action against the journalist Mylius in order to discredit the story (and incidentally to discredit the belief that 'royalty cannot answer back').

When the London wholesalers declined a book or withdrew it and their Scottish counterparts failed to do so, the clean-up crusaders had a field-day in the press. In connection with a 'flagrant and obscene' novel of 1908, a leading article complimented Smith's and Wyman's on their 'wholesome respect for the law' and went on:

'The lessees of the Scottish rail-way bookstalls are apparently not so particular.'

But the Scottish press was always ready to champion its own:

'Hearty and well-deserved compliments to the peculiarly Scottish firm of Messrs John Menzies & Co. The "cool business regard" and "wholesome respect for the law" which actuated those English firms are all very well in their way, but the high moral sense, which is the outcome of a wholesome Scottish upbringing on porridge and the Shorter

'British vulgarity asserted itself.' Strait-laced customers might object, but the comic postcard was an item of stock no bookstall could afford to be without.

SHE: I GO TO BED BETWEEN TEN AND ELEVEN."
HE: "TUT! TOO MANY IN A BED."

"WHICH IS THE QUICKEST WAY FOR ME TO GET TO THE POST OFFICE?"
"ROLL SIR."

Catechism is better. . . . Let (the leader writer) try if he can get any questionable book at any of Messrs Menzies's bookstalls. If he succeeds, he has only to report the matter to the clerk in charge. He will not accomplish the feat a second time.'

Censorship to the wholesaler, on whose doorstep all complaints land, signifies a delicate balancing act between good taste and profitability. Its history reveals how permissiveness (or, as some would say, enlightenment) spreads and is brought up short–the seaside postcards, music-hall songs and titillating drivel of 'society' journals in late Edwardian days would be unacceptable today, for example; and how, on the whole, it keeps pace with the increasing broadmindedness of the customer. Charles Eason of Dublin adopted a typically Irish compromise:

'I thought a good deal upon the question . . . which was forced on me in the case of several books which I found distinctly pernicious and immoral.... Some were withdrawn from sale, and others were not again exposed, but on enquiry the public were warned of the character of the works and, if persistently asked for, they were procured for them in most instances.'

Formerly the wrath of the virtuous was turned against literature which portrayed or advocated a degrading way of life. Then, with the arrival of D. H. Lawrence and James Joyce, the criticisms centred on explicit acts or rude words. During the First World War many people complained to Menzies's about the 'foul and corrupting novels' displayed on bookstalls, implying that soldiers who read them would forget the noble ideals for which they fought. Concern for the soldiers was voiced again in the Second World War. The Archbishop of Glasgow, in a letter to Colonel Charles:

'. . . It is indeed sad to think that our brave sailors put their lives at stake to bring to our shores these American weapons directly calculated to corrupt youth and destroy souls.'

By 'American weapons' he meant the crime-and-sex paperbacks–*No Orchids for Miss Blandish* and the like–which sold by the hundred thousand and brightened many a dreary rail journey. Menzies' manager at the Glasgow Central bookstall could only plead that

'in my experience the troops want literature that is exciting and spicy'.

Spicy indeed by comparison are the girlie magazines on sale in the 1980s which continually raise problems for the wholesalers. Menzies's have made serious efforts over a long period to devise formulae which will safeguard their managers, protect their reputation and at the same time give the public what it asks for. The firm's lawyers and retail executives examine all such material as a matter of course before it is put on display.

Magazines which appear to overstep the blurred line are withdrawn. Magazines which habitually publish potentially libellous material are not handled at all. Then the offenders air their grievances, issuing statements to press, radio and television. Despairing of satisfying both puritans and liberals, the firm can only point to the practical realities:

'We do not see our role as being one of censors, but our managers are at risk and we must protect them against the possibility of prosecution.'

The financial penalties are not the worst of it. If you are a suburban newsagent or village shopkeeper–particularly if you happen to live in Scotland–it is no joke to be branded for life as The Man who Sold the Dirty Book.

8

'Open for business as usual'

'Open for business as usual'

In the arts columns of the newspapers Augustus John and Stanley Spencer are news. At the circulating libraries an unknown writer called Nevil Shute is praised, but the author of the day is Erich Maria Remarque (*All Quiet on the Western Front*). In the drama columns you can read how London crowds flock to R. C. Sheriff's *Journey's End*. On the gossip pages the names of Noel Coward, Ivor Novello and Tallulah Bankhead crop up and Mrs Kate Meyrick and her red-haired daughters are forever in court, defending their Silver Slipper and Forty-Three night clubs. The papers say it's time the Prince of Wales got married. D. H. Lawrence completes *Lady Chatterley's Lover* (a book the wholesalers will *not* handle) and writes a piece for the *Daily Express* entitled 'Is England Still a Man's Country?'

With only his wife to wave farewell, a maverick Australian called Bert Hinkler takes off from Croydon in a single-engined aircraft and lands at Darwin fifteen days later, having halved the time for the England-Australia flight.

This is 1928. Western Europe crawls to recovery after the greatest war she has known. Across the Atlantic one sensational boom follows another– oil, grain, real estate, automobile–and Mr Rockefeller says America is breezing irresistibly along to an 'era of prosperity which will far transcend anything the world has ever known'. He is not aware that, about a year from now, the carefree tunes of the jazz-and-ballyhoo epoch will be replaced with the lugubrious 'Buddy, Can You Spare a Dime?'

Economists blame the General Strike of 1926 for Britain's failure to make a complete recovery after the war. As a total shutdown it lasted only a few days but, coming when it did, when the nation was struggling to regain a foothold in world markets, it was serious. Britain muddles on, increasing imports, decreasing exports, remaining obsessed with traditional methods of business. In 1928, for the first time in recorded history, her invisible earnings (from foreign investments, shipping and financial services) have failed to make good the loss on her balance of trade.

In the newspaper and associated businesses, black clouds of uncertainty and stock-exchange panics had a glint of silver: public anxieties meant more special editions, a greater demand for news. (Drama brought additional revenue, but put the system under additional strain. Letters of appreciation in the firm's files for 1936, for example, refer to 'the extra work and worry in regard to despatching newspapers in connection with the death of the late King George V'.)

An encouraging memorandum went round Menzies's staff, telling them no dismissals were contemplated. After the General Strike the company, unlike most companies, was able to assure everyone that wages, hours and conditions of service would be maintained at the pre-1926 level. What was more, there would be a fortnight's holiday with pay (quite a rare benefit fifty-odd years ago) and employees off work through illness would receive a proportion of their wages from the firm (another revolutionary concession).

In 1928, which is again described as a 'troublous year', Menzies's set up a notable landmark in staff relations and working conditions. The company pensions scheme was such a remarkable innovation that it required a good deal of explanatory literature. It was, as the introductory leaflet put it, 'a free gift from the directors to the staff', a non-contributory arrangement by which anyone who had been with the company for fifteen years qualified

Charles Cuthbert Menzies, a boyhood picture.
Charles was the artistic member of Colonel Charles's family, a musician and a collector of rare books. He died in 1951, aged forty-six.

for retirement payments based on salary and length of service. An employee who had been forty years at work and was earning £4 a week or more when he retired could count on a pension of £2 a week for life.

'He', not 'she'. Female staff, with the exception of certain manageresses, were not normally admitted to the pensions scheme. They were not included until 1952.

Compared with the earnings-related and index-linked awards and the old-age benefits of the present day, it looks a modest enough hand-out. For the 1920s it was an exciting novelty and a generous gesture (even members of trades unions were eligible, so long as the affairs of their union were judged to be 'conducive to the interests of the company') and with it John Menzies & Company Ltd established a precedent which many other companies considered extremely dangerous.

Shadows of the imminent Depression fell first across the station book-stalls. Their gross receipts for 1928 on the L.M.&S. routes, which now covered most of Scotland and the west-coast routes from London, were £510,000. Next year they were £494,000 and the year after that £478,000: small reductions, but significant in an area which had consistently shown upward trends. When the railway companies started behaving with ingratiating politeness the wholesalers knew the slump had arrived. In 1931 the L.M.&S. actually offered John Menzies's all the bookstall contracts south of Carlisle. "It is not intended to ask for formal tenders," they said.

Menzies's replied that they couldn't think of expanding south of the Border. John R. sent a copy of his letter to his friend Sir William Acland, who dealt with all the W.H. Smith & Son franchises. Menzies's had recently confirmed new leases for all the Scottish stations, he said, "but the turnover is still falling". Acland wrote:

'It was nice of you to write in the way you did, and we all appreciate the spirit very much. . . . We are glad of course to learn your answer about not going south, because we have always set our faces against the temptation to invade *your* territory.'

Throughout the firm's history, dark periods for commerce and country have generally brought changes at the top which, at the time, Menzies's could have well done without. In 1927 John R., chief architect of the company's fortunes since 1879, gave up the managing directorship to his brother Colonel Charles.

Another Menzies generation, the third, had appeared. Family history repeated itself. Colonel Charles's two sons, another John and another Charles, had come into the firm. Charles the younger brother was a director by 1930; his elder brother John had joined his father on the board three years earlier. "He had," says a senior member of the firm who knew him, "his father's and his grandfather's gift of enjoying work and he had a really first-class financial brain."

During a relatively short career with his father at the head of the company–only thirteen years–John ('John Francis') helped erect some notable milestones on the Menzies highway. He launched the pensions scheme and holidays-with-pay. He was involved in getting the railway bookstall leases agreed on a percentage basis. He secured the important concession of 1930 which permitted Menzies's to sell fruits and confectionery at their bookstalls wherever there were no other fruits-and-sweets sellers at the station.

John Francis Menzies, elder son of Colonel Charles and father of the present chairman. John Francis was vice-chairman of the firm when he died suddenly at the age of forty.

He established the gold-watch award: the firm's gift, of great value then, to employees who completed their forty years of service. (For a long time there was keen competition to see who could win it youngest, until Robert Crichton qualified at the age of fifty-one-and-a-half, setting a record unlikely ever to be broken.)

And John Francis and his father brought to an end an auld duel with that redoubtable bailie of Glasgow who had defended his little enclave so tenaciously for so long. Sir Robert Graham died and Menzies's took over the bookstall leases of the former Glasgow & South-western (then the L.M.&S.) Railway Company.

A picture taken between the wars. Some of the Menzies staff at work on the firm's accounts. This room in the head offices in Hanover Buildings, Edinburgh, with an electric lamp above each desk, was considered a spacious and elegant working environment in its day.

Along with the railway companies, the firm saw with some apprehension a wider conflict developing. Britain's road transport services were making inroads on country routes where the railways had known no competition. There was little the railway companies could do about it, apart from forbidding Menzies's to sell bus timetables at station bookstalls. That conflict, coupled with the long coal strike of 1930, hit rail passenger services disastrously. Against a background of branch-line closures and huge reductions in staff and overheads the L.M.&S. came cap in hand to their bookstall tenants, offering to renew leases at reduced rents.

John Francis and his father had other things on their minds. A profitable business in the long term was always the Menzies aim and, while other companies retrenched and sought to cut losses, Menzies's opened four new wholesale businesses (Kirkcaldy, Falkirk, Motherwell and Dumfries) and set up two new bookshops (Inverness and Aberdeen)—the first bookshops they owned outside Edinburgh, the precursors of a nationwide network of Menzies shops.

An expensive new warehouse in Dundee, much bigger than the old one, commanded the admiration of the *Evening Telegraph:*

'It is a building in the best modern manner, and the cheerful light interior would delight the heart of the most pessimistic person.'

While all that went on, father and son conducted the firm past a notable anniversary: 1933, the Menzies centenary. Tributes flowed in from all quarters—from national newspapers and magazines, from rival whole-salers, from the newsagents' federations and from publishers. (John Murray

of Albemarle Street said how much he and his authors owed 'to the kindly help of John Menzies—without them, who could really reach the heart of the Scottish reader?')

Such anniversaries naturally attract polite notices, but one theme runs through the shoals of congratulations: the sincere and unfailing courtesy, in good times and bad (setting aside the founder's little foibles, no doubt), which characterised Menzies's business attitudes down the ages. The National Bank of Scotland stated that for ninety-six of those hundred years they'd held the Menzies account and had never had a qualm or a cross word.

On a map of the Menzies kingdom in the middle 1930s the Highlands and Lowlands of Scotland are peppered with red dots. They are the station bookstalls, most densely congregated in the central belt, from Ayr through Glasgow and Edinburgh to Fife; scattered also among the towns and

"AULD REEKIE"

IN
SEARCH OF SCOTLAND
BY
H. V. MORTON

WITH 16 ILLUSTRATIONS AND A MAP

A chield's amang you takin' notes,
And faith he'll prent it.
—ROBERT BURNS

TENTH EDITION

BRIGHT
DAY

A NOVEL BY

J.B.
PRIESTLEY

In the 1930s, hardback books were the firm's major source of profit, next to newspapers and magazines. Before embarking, the average long-distance rail traveller bought his book for the journey and, as often as not, left it on the seat in the compartment at his destination. Thus the fame of authors such as H. V. Morton and J. B. Priestley was spread throughout the land.

villages, along all the rural railways, from those which penetrate the ragged promontories of the north-west to those which accompany the Border streams, hurrying down to the Tweed.

There are red dots in the sea. They're marked 'Ardrishaig steamers', 'Rothesay steamers', 'Ailsa Craig steamers' . . . the bookstalls on board the paddle-boats, replacements for the two-legged bookstalls of old, the sea-going basket boys. (In after years the Menzies bookstall was a first fitting in passenger boats, designed and built with the ship.)

The northernmost red dot is Thurso, the southernmost Silloth in Cumberland.

The map is also green-dotted, not so thickly; chiefly around Edinburgh's suburbs and the Waverley route through the knitwear towns to Carlisle. These are John Menzies kiosks, sited at wayside stations and halts which don't rate a full-scale bookstall.

Black dots, fifteen in all, represent branch warehouses and news distributing centres. Colonel Charles might remember his father's first tentative Glasgow 'experiment' with a branch—the Colonel was nine at the time. Now he's seventy-four, white-moustached, and he still pays annual visits to all the branches: Edinburgh, Leith, Glasgow, Paisley, Greenock, Kilmarnock, Dumfries, Motherwell, Falkirk, Dunfermline, Kirkcaldy, Perth, Dundee, Aberdeen and Inverness.

Three purple dots, one of them ancient and the other two modern: the Menzies shops in Edinburgh, Aberdeen and Inverness.

If we could pass that map slowly through a time-warp down future years, we'd see a few dots of red appearing but many more disappearing, as the railway branch lines are closed down. The black dots would spread steadily outwards, increasing both in number and size. The green dots would gradually vanish. The three purple dots would multiply at an amazing rate, until Scotland (and England too, if the map showed it) was a mass of them. Menzies's future lies among these retail establishments. As time goes by the firm will accelerate the process of building, buying up and taking over properties large and small, from famous bookshops to decaying one-man village stores, and turning them into cornucopias of books, magazines, newspapers, records and cassettes, sweets, tobacco and fancy goods under the blue-and-white John Menzies sign.

Between the wars it was no longer possible for headquarters to maintain the old personal contact with all the firm's outlets. Menzies's therefore recruited a corps of inspectors who travelled the country and submitted their reports. A sample from the late 1930s:

'Space is limited, though adequate for present needs . . . X gave me the impression as a very capable manager, though his appearance is slightly against him, unfortunately . . . general appearance of the warehouse is drab and could be brightened up with a coat of paint . . . this branch serves a poor locality but has a very good turnover . . . great difficulty will be experienced in procuring new premises in this area. . . .'

–from which we can see that, besides keeping up the efficient attitude to business which people expected of a Menzies establishment, the inspectors (former shop or bookstall managers themselves as a rule) were on the look-out for expansion potential.

By the time World War II broke out, all the bookstall leases except those in Aberdeen had been arranged on a percentage basis. In that city Menzies's took a twelve-year lease at £900 a year and profited handsomely, thanks to the extraordinary increases in turnover which the war brought about.

Books were still the company's chief commodity, if no longer the company's *raison d'être*. As the decade ended Menzies's were displaying Hodder's Ninepenny Novels (Ruby M. Ayres was the darling of this range) at the cheap end, and the works of Francis Brett Young, John Buchan, E.M. Delafield, Naomi Jacob and J.B. Priestley costing about 7/6 (37½p) at the expensive end. Best-selling authors of 1939 were H.V. Morton (*In Search of Scotland*), Axel Munthe and A.J. Cronin–on the Scottish bookstalls, that is.

Retiring after forty-three years' service at the Glasgow Central bookstall, Tom Johnston remembered when customers clamoured for Ouida and Mrs Henry Wood. "Now the women read the men's books," he said, "and you get schoolgirls asking for boys' papers." Johnston knew to a hair how many copies a new book would sell; or thought he did. He wagered a bottle of champagne that he'd sell a thousand copies of *Masel'* (Harry Lauder's autobiography) in three days when it first came out. He managed only nine hundred and ninety-seven and lost the bet.

Johnston was typical of the old-style Menzies hand who wore the good name of the firm like a precious diadem. His dedication had been such, even as a youngster, that when they sent him to the Oban bookstall he thought he'd better learn the Gaelic and he went for lessons from the best authority, Professor Blackie. "But he failed miserably," Johnston told a staff meeting, "because I could never master more than a couple of sentences, one of them being 'Get your claes aff and get intae your bed'."

Two other stalwarts of the country districts retired about the same time. George Henderson had managed the Tay Bridge bookstall. In boyhood days he'd travelled the Perth-Kingussie line, selling papers for a wage of two shillings (10p) a week, setting out daily on the first morning train with a basket of *Daily Mirrors* and *Daily Sketches* and cigarettes of various brands, plus his newspaper and magazine parcels for retailers en route. The boys were adept at flinging small packets into signal-boxes and the doorways of lineside cottages. A friend of Henderson's tossed a sack so high in the excess of his exuberance that it wrapped itself round the wires overhead and stopped all the trains. Taken before a magistrate, he was released with a reprimand, on condition that 'he would never do it again'. He told Henderson that if he tried for a lifetime he didn't think he could do it again.

The other retirement was that of James Baird, whom we met earlier, round the piano. He'd graduated along a well-trodden Menzies promotion path: assistant at Glasgow Central, manager at Oban, manager at Aberdeen, finally manager at Carlisle. His young days at the bookstalls were an age of elegance, when publishers' representatives paid their calls in white gloves and that magisterial figure, the inspector of bookstalls, turned up in a top hat. On such occasions Baird was sent to the station refreshment rooms for "three cups of tea and a saucer, the inspector's here today"–which prompted the invariable response: "Oh, drinks out of a saucer, does he?"

Henderson, Baird and Johnston notched up a hundred and forty-eight years of service between them. They were, along with many others, the backbone of the organisation, the solid base on which the company's fortunes rested; even though things were no longer done, in their opinion, the way they used to be done. Rosy memories coloured past experience. James Leckie always swore that the pre-1914 covered wagons of the transport fleet gave no trouble at all, while the modern vans were in and out of the workshops all the time. Human stature had diminished too:

"In those days, d'ye ken, only the ladies and gentlemen of the comfortable classes bought magazines and travelled on trains. Nowadays you find all sorts doing it."

In the late 1930s and early 1940s a job with Menzies's was an attractive prospect for a boy or girl in a provincial town. "A job with John Menzies," they used to say, "is a job for life." Boys of sixteen started at 15/- a week (75p) and that had increased to £3 by the time they were twenty-six. Girls entered at 14/- (70p) and reached their maximum of £2 at the age of twenty-four. (These were about the same rates as those paid to young people in the local authority's service.)

Asked why girls earned less than boys for the same kind of job, the employer's short answer was that "the boy must save money in order to marry the girl".

When the boy departed on war service his service pay was made up to the civilian level. A Menzies warehouseman who left in 1940 with 22/- a week (£1.10) came back in 1945 to £4.5.0 a week (£4.25); the normal increments having been added. In another five years the £4.5.0 had gone up to £10, well ahead of the national average. City staff, particularly at the higher levels, were exceptionally well paid by the standards of the day. At the Glasgow branch in 1946 the *assistant* manager earned £1,000 a year.

Conscious of his dignity and the responsibilities of his office, the bookstall manager awaits his customers. This picture is dated 1935.

The firm had a fairly quiet war. Head office in Edinburgh laid its contingency plans, duplicating its records and preparing alternative premises in various areas to which the branches might move if bombed out. Bookstalls were considered particularly vulnerable targets: they were dotted along the railway lines which made a gleaming flight path, by day or night, for enemy aircraft. But out of a hundred and fifty or so only three were hit: the Partick (Glasgow) stall destroyed, the stalls at Greenock and Fraserburgh stations slightly damaged; no casualties.

The annihilation of British cities which everyone expected at the start of the war did not take place. Menzies's only serious loss was at Greenock on the Clyde. On 7th May 1941 manager James Kyle arrived to find his warehouse a smoking ruin from the raid of the previous night:

'Stock, magazine and news lists, ledgers, furniture, barrows, cash register, clock and typewriter had vanished . . . the safe was found after a twenty-four-hour search . . we ripped off the back and found nothing but the steel binders of the ledgers, pound notes reduced to powder, and silver and copper coins burned black. . . .'

After a survey of the devastation Mr Kyle went off to queue for several hours at the only telephone kiosk in action to report to Edinburgh.

For a branch manager it was a catastrophe too deep for tears when his warehouse, with its records and multifarious news lists and other vital ingredients of the complex distribution service, built up over many years, was reduced to rubble. A direct hit on the Edinburgh headquarters would have paralysed the whole company; but Edinburgh survived intact. The firewatchers' log tells of tedious uneventful nights on the roof and upper floors of Hanover Buildings:

'Nothing to report . . . no biscuits again . . . police called about black-out … nothing to report.'

For the vast majority of Menzies's shops, branches, bookstalls and kiosks it was, in the jargon of the times, 'business as usual'. That slogan reappeared at Greenock one day when the authorities shut down Princes Pier, the place where the trains met the Clyde steamers. A newspaper photograph reproduced the sign:

'THIS STATION IS COMPLETELY CLOSED TO THE PUBLIC AND ALL ENTRY, UNDER ANY CIRCUMSTANCES WHATEVER, IS EXPRESSLY FORBIDDEN. BOOKSTALL ON PLATFORM OPEN FOR BUSINESS AS USUAL.'

The ordinary hazards of bookstall life continued. Robberies were more frequent in the black-out and pilfering increased. At Musselburgh station on New Year's Day 1941 a girl assistant was killed when a goods train ploughed into the bookstall.

On the lighter side of war's alarms, an elephant came to the Aberdeen station bookstall and offered a coin for a magazine–and made a clean sweep of the literature on display when it waved goodbye with its trunk. It was part of the advance publicity for a theatrical company.

Also from Aberdeen (for some reason a regular source of unlikely happenings) came the tale of the girl who put her evening dress into the cleaner's before the victory-celebration dinner-dance. It couldn't be found and she was on her way to the dance in a borrowed one when she saw it pinned across the newsagent's window with WELCOME HOME SANDY painted on it.

Critical days for the nation were paralleled, as so often in the past, by

'She was very brave to take us on.' Mrs Menzies, née Helen Frances Aitken, came into the firm on the death of her son John Francis. When her husband Colonel Charles died three years later she replaced him as chairman and held the post for eight years.

critical days for the house of Menzies. Under a succession of domestic crises such as its leadership had to contend with, a more rigid and less well-conducted structure might have collapsed.

John Francis Menzies died suddenly in 1940. His father Colonel Charles came back into harness, though he was eighty-two. Three years later he too was dead and the firm took the unusual step of inviting his widow to replace him: the first woman director and the only one in a hundred and fifty years of Menzies history. The idea was to preserve the name of Menzies at the top until the next descendant of the founder should be old enough to assume the burden. ('Young' Charles was in the Royal Air Force and 'very young' John was still at school.)

Mrs Menzies was no figurehead, but a person of spirit, important to the firm. "Looking back," says an ex-director, "I always thought she was very brave to take us on."

More important, however, in unsettled times were Menzies's senior executives: men like Peter Nisbet, first company secretary and right-hand man of John R. and Colonel Charles (he died in 1940); James Roberston, former bookstalls inspector who became managing director; James Anderson who succeeded him as managing director in 1946; Reginald Nussey, a younger man but long in the firm's service, who was to end up as managing director of John Menzies (Holdings) in 1959; and, also after the war, H.M. Graham, a vice-chairman for sixteen years. In those senior executives and others like them the esprit and accumulated wisdom of the company resided; and the old ship held her course.

From 1948 to 1951 John Maxwell Menzies, great grandson of the founder, was going through the departments, gaining experience. In 1951 he took over the chairmanship from his grandmother. His thirty-two years at the helm since that date have been a progressive realisation of the ambitious desires of his forebears; and more.

Over in Glasgow, at the Central station bookstall, an old man named Edward Murdoch moved towards his retirement. He had served the firm in that most demanding of bookstall jobs for more than half a century. When he went, the last physical link with pre-incorporation days (pre-1906) was broken. And an entirely new era was just beginning.

Problem with a pachyderm. When circus elephants come off the train at Aberdeen, they instinctively make for the station bookstall for a browse.

9

'If dry, leave paper in doorway'

'If dry, leave paper in doorway'

'Grateful thanks to the kiosk attendant at Pitlochry station, who has brought us our papers without fail this bitter winter.'

Such tributes were not uncommon in the personal columns of a Highland newspaper. A harsh climate gives customers opportunities to see how much hardship and heroism are involved in the miracle of the daily delivery. In those quiet places the householder has time to reflect on the course of events which brings him the newspapers. A flat-dweller in the centre of Glasgow may take it all for granted. The grateful recipient at Pitlochry, however, witnessed only the last scene of a logistical operation of astonishing complexity: a boy or girl from the railway station down by the river, plodding uphill in the snow.

Some lingering excitement of travel and communications, some trace of the old romance of road and rail, still attaches to the nightly drama of the newspapers. It's a large drama, with a cast of hundreds. The advent of other media–radio, television–has not diminished the circulation of newspapers throughout Great Britain. Per capita it's the highest in the world, and it continues to increase.

British newspapers come into three categories: national dailies, evening papers, local papers. The principal publishing centres for national and evening editions are London and Manchester for the whole of the United Kingdom; Edinburgh, Glasgow and Dundee (stronghold of the important Thomson-Leng organisation) for Scotland. From those five cities several million items must find their way every night, in the space of a few hours, into several million homes. The wealth and glory of the tycoons, from Northcliffe and Beaverbrook to Murdoch and Matthews, and the reputations and livelihoods of columnists and reporters, have long been in the hands of those who distribute their products. As Sir Robert Graham pointed out, what is not sold today is unlikely to be sold tomorrow.

The nightly drama of the news: 1, loading the Menzies vans; 2, making up the bundles for retailers; 3, packed, stacked and ready for despatch.

A newspaper's very existence depends on providing late news at an early hour. Over the years the interval between its coming off the presses and dropping through the subscriber's letterbox has been reduced to a minimum. Some links in the chain along which it moves demand critical timing—and that is where the wholesale distributor of long standing, who has spent a hundred years refining and tightening up the machinery, has the advantage. There have been many improvements in the routine since the *Northern Chronicle* of 1898 said of John Menzies's:

'Prompt despatch is the secret of their success.'

The first editions of nearly all the London dailies are in the loading bays of their publishing buildings by 9.30 p.m. the previous day. They are made up in bundles of about forty-two pounds apiece, which represents ten dozen newspapers of normal size. An armada of delivery vans takes the bales by the thousand to the various distribution centres of the capital, for the London area, and to various railheads for the provinces and Scotland. The trip takes only a few minutes: it's no accident that the mass-circulation proprietors seized bases in areas like the Grays Inn Road, a stone's-throw from Euston, King's Cross and St Pancras stations, the departure points for the northern expresses. If they were setting up bases today they'd be sited closer to Heathrow, for newspapers increasingly travel by air.

Let us follow the adventures, any time these past twenty years, of the few hundred bales which are coming out of Fleet Street, Farringdon Street and the Grays Inn Road and are labelled for MENZIES EDINBURGH. Ordinarily the vans take them to Heathrow, arriving there in time for the 11.40 p.m. flight. (Timings alter, but not significantly.)

The bales reach Turnhouse, the airport for Edinburgh, about one a.m. and vans are waiting to pick them up and transport them seven miles to the city, to Menzies's warehouse. On the same flight, bound for other Menzies

4, Vehicles on the starting-grid, and the early-morning grand prix about to get under way.

A few of the daily papers whose several editions and enormous print runs are handled in the complicated night operations of the news distributors. A greater number and variety of newspapers is produced in Britain, and they travel faster to their destinations, than anywhere else in the world.

warehouses in lowland Scotland by van or rail, are bales labelled Perth, Dundee, Dunfermline, Kirkcaldy, Falkirk, Stirling, Dumfries and Galashiels. Bales for Aberdeen and Inverness and points north are on the Heathrow-Glasgow flight and will probably be routed on from Glasgow by air.

But our concern is with the Edinburgh consignment. It's now four a.m. and Menzies's make-up crew at the warehouse has split the bales into smaller parcels for the city, the outskirts and the country districts. The first van takes off, to a Midlothian mining village. Others follow, bound for remote communities of the Lammermuir and Moorfoot hills. They're small orders, they get away quickly. Some vans go only as far as the Edinburgh railway stations or the bus station. Much of the distribution to retailers is done by early-morning buses and local trains; even by taxi. If, in the half-light of dawn, you see a taxi going down the road and wonder what's afoot it will be a taxi from the city warehouse, perhaps delivering a single copy of the *Guardian* for a small newsagent's only *Guardian* customer, because that morning the *Guardian* came in late and missed the general delivery.

This sort of thing happens chiefly with newspapers which publish in Manchester and make their journey to Edinburgh, Glasgow or Perth on special trains. A typical 'news special' leaves Manchester about 11 p.m., unloads at eight stations en route and ends up in Perth about 5.30 a.m. At Carlisle, Stirling and Perth the Menzies staff are waiting for it and they deal with newspapers for those areas at their local distributing centre. On the special trains there have been experiments in processing–sorting, making up, labelling–during the journey; but this doesn't occur in Scotland.

One of the newspapers which earned the Pitlochry customer's gratitude would have come to Scotland by air or special train, to be processed in Edinburgh or Perth. It would have been among a score of newspaper packages put on the Inverness train, one of the bundles to be tossed out at halts on the stations of the route. Menzies's kiosk attendant would have caught it–about nine o'clock of an icy morning, perhaps. He'd have separated the paper from other papers in the bundle, put it in a wrapper for personal delivery and, there being no more trains for a while, would have taken it up by hand to the listed address.

Crossing the England-Scotland flow of newsprint at dead of night there is, of course, a Scotland-England flow; not to mention intersecting currents of newspapers within those countries. Papers are published in Aberdeen and Dundee, for example, and are on sale in Glasgow and Edinburgh first thing in the morning. Scottish newspapers going south arrive by special train in Manchester at 5.15 a.m. and by another special train in London at 5.45 a.m.–or they may do. They may arrive earlier, on passenger trains. Menzies's have devised numerous options and an impressive back-up system to take account of delayed flights, breakdowns, frozen points and industrial troubles.

The sort of split-second timing that warehouse staff and drivers worked to was illustrated in the case of the *Scotsman* newspaper going to England. For many years it rolled off the presses in Edinburgh at 10.45 p.m. nightly, spent three minutes on the overhead conveyor to the loading bays and two minutes in the vans to the Waverley station; and was dumped on board as the 10.50 p.m. train to York pulled out. A porter lamented the introduction of diesels in the 1960s: "They're no use, they're too quick off the mark. With the steam trains you could run alongside, throwing the bales in."

Sending the *Scotsman* to Glasgow was a dreamy affair by comparison. It caught the 11 p.m. train, so the despatch staff had a whole fifteen minutes to get the bales to the station.

Multiply the Edinburgh warehouse's ordered chaos, as the station and airport collections come in and go out again, by eighty-seven, and we have a picture of the Menzies organisation at its midnight exercises: there are eighty-seven wholesale houses and warehouses. The weight of newsprint handled nightly in Edinburgh alone is twenty-five tons: fifteen hundred bales to be broken up and reassembled in the shape of eight hundred parcels for retailers large and small. (Nationwide, the firm supplies twelve thousand newsagents with thirty-five million papers and magazines per week.)

Menzies's have their own fleet of delivery vans. Up to thirty hundredweight they're standard commercial vehicles. Above that size they have Menzies-designed bodywork. Of the six hundred-odd vans used for deliveries, about half are hired with their drivers, local men who know their territories and have tuned their routines very finely. Take the old night shuttle, Edinburgh and Dumfries. The vans left from either end, delivering packages to retailers en route, and met at Abington, the mid-point of their journey. There the drivers exchanged vans and continued with deliveries in the reverse direction; and returned to their starting-points. The two centres are seventy miles apart, with bleak moorland in between, difficult in winter weather. If one driver missed his rendezvous the other would drive ten miles towards him and then, if they'd still not met, would turn back and telephone headquarters.

If we could see all the Menzies journeys, night after night, plotted on a chart they would resemble a large piece of fine lace; and to trace the voyage of one newspaper to its destination would be like tracing the ins and outs of a ball of wool. Follow a thread to its farthest limits and we'll probably end up at a Highland village store–the kind of place which sells lettuces, mittens, souvenir pottery, milk and biscuits and bottles of wine and which– since it holds the Menzies agency–boasts a list of maybe half a dozen customers. The little store is very likely run by a sturdy individualist with his own way of doing things. He's probably never met the van driver who penetrates to his fastness while the countryside sleeps, but they communicate through third parties–the postman, perhaps–and through bits of paper pinned to the shop door. When the van driver hands over to another van driver, there's a lot of local knowledge to be handed over too, such as:

'Maclachlan, Arrochar: if dry, leave paper in doorway, if wet, take it up the next passage and leave in second coalbox on left.'

The daily papers, of course, are only part of the story. Weekly and monthly magazines add to the bulk and diversity of the freight and bring

Magazines large and small, imposing and humble, weekly and monthly, designed for all ages and tastes, festoon the shop shelves and bookstalls in glittering array. Now and again a famous old title disappears, but new ones, appearing at the rate of two or three a month, more than make up the deficiency.

their own complexities to the operations. The quality magazines and penny-number periodicals which the founder knew are no more, but a vastly increased output has taken their place. You have only to glance along the range of reading matter at a Menzies shop or bookstall to see a range that would have left the old-timers quite bewildered, and wondering where, even in a great city, enough people could find time to read them all. The most modest rural newsagent now displays a rack of periodicals which, earlier this century, would have been more than a city bookseller could have coped with: paperbacks, do-it-yourself and hobbies magazines, women's magazines, leisure and sporting magazines and special interest literature of every description.

To attack the bookstall or the newsagent has continued to be a popular pastime. Like the railways and the postal services, they're a broad area in which people expect perfection–people, that is, who never stop to think what wonderful services they take for granted. Still, if John Menzies's cared to, they could have built up a volume of press cuttings over the past thirty years to prove that some do stop to think, and to admire, and to offer bouquets. A Glasgow evening paper:

'Where are the slickest sales assistants in this city? They are the assistants at John Menzies's Queen Street station bookstall. They lip-read your order, observe what money you have in your hand, pass you your papers and take the money in one hand, giving change with the other, all in one movement!'

Another Glasgow paper welcomed the new-style Menzies bookstall when it was introduced at St Enoch's station in May 1950:

'A first-class little bookshop, a kind of literary grotto . . . brilliant lighting . . . a much-needed touch of brightness in otherwise dull and drab surroundings.'

Brightness was the hallmark of a Menzies stall. The firm never skimped on electricity. Many travellers noticed how the bookstall's lively appearance emphasised the depressing atmosphere of its surroundings. In 1964 the *Daily Mail* set out on a search for Scotland's most dreadful railway station. The search ended in Fife; and Kirkcaldy was proclaimed the place that passengers would least like to be stranded at. But even there the citation of gloom was relieved with mention of:

'a cheery-looking bookstall, trying vainly to beat its surroundings'.

Bright lights and pleasing colours, an air of life and activity: such, since World War II, have been the outward manifestations of a forward-looking organisation, both at its bookstalls and in its retail shops. Menzies's are not the only shopkeepers with a century and more of musty, slow-paced tradition behind them, but they were the first in Scotland to appreciate that warm, well-carpeted, well-lighted establishments were good for the morale of shoppers and staff; and therefore good for business too.

Nationalisation of the United Kingdom's railways involved the reappraisal and renegotiation of hundreds of bookstall franchises. Over the British Isles, the situation at the time of the new agreements of 1953 was much the same as it had been in the 1930s. Eason's of Dublin had a monopoly in the Republic of Ireland and held some Northern Ireland stations too. Menzies's controlled the region between Carlisle and the far north; Wyman's had a substantial but scattered stake in the Midlands of England and the West Country and on the North Wales coast; W. H. Smith &

Son, the largest bookstall company in the world, shared the Midlands with Wyman's and held unchallenged most of the Southern and Eastern regions of what was then called British Railways.

Under the 1953 revisions Menzies's secured in Scotland the leases of seventy-three bookstalls and three kiosks; and in England two bookstalls (Carlisle and Silloth) and two kiosks (Carlisle and Berwick-upon-Tweed). The range of permitted merchandise was extended. Menzies bookstalls now sold newspapers, magazines, stationery, camera film, tobacco and other smokers' requisites, fancy goods and leather goods; and they had the privilege of operating slot machines and of using wheeled trolleys on the platforms. (The wheeled trolley was a refinement of the basket boy's barrow. Menzies had produced it in the 1930s. It had been withdrawn during the war and the Mark II Menzies trolley was first seen at Glasgow Central station in 1954.)

The new contracts required bookstall staff to wear a uniform type of hat or an armband of a conspicuous colour. They were allowed to use trains, as of old, free of charge, for transporting equipment and sending parcels to other bookstalls and returning newspapers and books. The British Transport Commission took an inclusive rental of £56,000 a year for the eighty stances: it was a reasonable figure, observing that for three-quarters of a century the larger Scottish bookstalls had been paying rentals of up to £1,000 apiece.

Bookstalls were no longer confined to railway stations. As long ago as 1934, at the first Royal Highland Show, held in Glasgow, John Menzies had built a bookstall. At the great Empire Exhibition of 1938 in Bellahouston Park, Glasgow, the John Menzies bookstall had been not the least of the attractions. Since the middle 1930s there had been bookstalls at bus stations. And for as long as most people could remember there had been bookstalls on board the steamers which took passengers down the Clyde and to and from Ireland and the western isles.

At Turnhouse near Edinburgh in 1948 the company opened its first airport bookstall. Within six years it had bookstalls at the airports of Renfrew (now Glasgow), Prestwick, Dalcross (Inverness) and Dyce (Aberdeen). Thirteen years after that Menzies's were allocated Unit number 1 in the plan for the modern airport at Turnhouse, but by that time the Prestwick stance had been combined with a post office and leased to Richard Douglas Ltd. To compensate for the closing-down of the Dyce bookstall, new stances were taken at the Newcastle and Leeds/Bradford airports.

Under the 1953 agreements Menzies's acquired Berwick-upon-Tweed from W.H. Smith's. Now the firm held the two rail gateways to Scotland. The news would have pleased Colonel Charles, had he been alive. He once sat in a railway compartment, travelling south through Berwick-upon-Tweed, and heard his English fellow-passengers agree how nice it was to see the old familiar 'Smith' replacing the strange and unpronounceable 'Menzies' on the bookstalls: it made them feel they were in civilisation once more.

A slight linguistic problem attached to the spread of the name 'Menzies' throughout Britain. Even Scots may be heard pronouncing it the way it is spelled. Country Scots often say 'Meenis'. As for the English, it's proved easier to establish the name on signboards throughout the land than to persuade more than a tiny minority to use the proper pronunciation. 'There are obvious disadvantages in a national organisation operating under a number of different names,' said the Menzies house magazine in 1967, when it announced that the one name would embrace all the subsidiaries; but that name still operates under a number of different pronunciations. The *Menzies Chronicle* went on:

'Perhaps this is a suitable occasion to impress on all concerned that the correct pronunciation of our name is MING ESS, accented on the MING.'

As an aid to memory, someone recalled a limerick:

'There was a young lady called Menzies
Who asked "Do you know what this thenzies?"
Her aunt with a gasp
Replied "It's a wasp,
And you're holding the end where the stenzies".'

On his way through Prestwick airport in 1956, Mr Robert Menzies, prime minister of Australia, stopped at the bookstall to buy a couple of who-dun-nits. He was wearing a tie of the Menzies dress tartan. Asked about a rumour that he couldn't bear to be called 'Ming Ess' he said that, on the contrary, he rather liked it.

It could be the opening scene of a Hitchcock film or a Simenon thriller . . . but it's only Carlisle station at night, during a lull between trains. When the Glasgow-Euston train steams in, the bookstall will spring to life. ('Steams' is the word: this picture was taken in 1949.)

10

'From Thurso to Penzance'

'From Thurso to Penzance'

John Maxwell Menzies. Since he became chairman in 1951, the firm has pursued a policy of vigorous expansion.

When the John Menzies chairman, in the firm's one-hundred-and-twenty-fifth birthday book (1958), said that many shops had fine traditions but that high overheads and increasing costs were forcing them to close down, he was referring specifically to Scottish bookshops; though the same applied to retail establishments generally. There was nothing new in that, nor anything unusual in successful businesses buying up unsuccessful ones: that was the law of competition by which mankind lived. As another Scot, Andrew Carnegie, had said many years before: "It is a harsh law but a necessary one, for it ensures the survival of the fittest, and that ensures progress." Without conflict and competition, we'd still be swinging through the trees.

Post-war economics merely accelerated the process.

Before the war, as we have seen, John Menzies had bought up a few companies which were in poor health and had reinvigorated them. To consider only those in the Menzies heartland, Princes Street, Edinburgh, known to Scots as the finest thoroughfare in the world: by the middle 1930s the firm had taken over MacNiven & Wallace, a bookshop established when the first John Menzies was an apprentice; and, at the other end of the street, the equally venerable house of Elliot.

But historically the tendency had been for large companies outside Scotland to acquire the ailing businesses. And now Menzies's were in a position to challenge the trend, and to think about reversing it. In the first twelve post-war years they opened twenty retail shops in different parts of Scotland, all on premises threatened with collapse, or a change of business, or a takeover by someone from England.

Faithful to the occupational traditions of the founder, Menzies's took the keenest interest in bookselling–in what, judging by the number of shops which came on to the market, looked like the decline and fall of the profession. Of such places the owners had often pursued the same business methods, in exactly the same quaint surroundings, as their Georgian and early-Victorian ancestors. It was remarkable they'd survived so long. When John Menzies acquired such a shop (as they did in Aberdeen, Inverness, Dundee, Falkirk, Perth, Oban, Paisley and Kilmarnock) they set about renovating and refitting the place and making it bright, spacious and comfortable for customers and staff. They took some trouble to preserve the essential character of peculiarly Scottish institutions (antlers, targes and bulls' heads for the Highlands); but 'quaint' was not in their vocabulary.

Those operations brought back a company whose name was identified with the bookstalls and news distribution to the career of the founder. John Menzies became a retail bookseller once more. By embracing a wider range of retail business they also recovered the title of stationer–the oldest title of all, a title derived from the eighteenth-century dealers in writing materials who first 'stationed' themselves on one spot instead of peddling their wares round the streets.

Almost as soon as John M. Menzies became chairman in 1951 a policy of expansion south of the Border had been decided on. Once adopted, it gathered momentum and proceeded at a rate which far exceeded the growth of the previous century.

In London, in 1955, the great wholesale house of Simpkin Marshall (to book distribution what Cunard had been to shipping) suddenly ceased trading. Wyman & Sons took over Simpkin Marshall's export business, but four years later the word went round that Wyman's themselves were being taken over. In April 1959 it was revealed that the 'mystery bidders' were John Menzies. The transfer involved Wyman's formidable wholesale GHQ in New Street Square, London; seventy-eight shops; and about two hundred bookstalls in London and the English provinces. Menzies's offered 15/- (75p) a share when Wyman's stood at 10/- (50p) and the acquisition, including liability for preference shares, cost them more than £1m. The printing side–Cox & Wyman–was then sold back to the former directors for about £½m.

Intrigued by the coup of a northern invader whom few had heard of, the *Investor's Chronicle* did some hasty research and briefed its readership on the obscure private company which had so swiftly conquered a well-known public one:

'Sassenachs cannot be expected to know the Menzies business, for it is a family business that has been jealously guarded for the century and a quarter that has elapsed since John Menzies opened his first shop in Princes Street, Edinburgh, in 1833. . . .

'(It) has wholesale distributing houses all over Scotland, 130 bookstalls on railway stations and at airports, 26 first-class bookshops and is the biggest firm of wholesale stationers in Scotland. An interesting sidelight on the Wyman bid is that Wyman's won the L.&N.W.R. and G.W.R. bookstall contracts from W.H. Smith earlier this century, a move that caused Smith's to establish its chain of retail shops. And it was Menzies that eventually took over the contract for the bookstall at Edinburgh's Waverley station five years after W.H. Smith gave up the tenancy in 1857.

'In acquiring one bookstall the company had to buy an entire railway station, and not only does the bookshop in Barnton station, Edinburgh, belong to the firm, but the platform and station buildings do too. . . .

'We have not heard the end of the House of Menzies. If precedent is any guide, expansion is not likely to end with the acquisition of Wyman's.'

Wyman's name, as we saw earlier, was associated with the railway stations in the Midlands of England, the West Country and on the North Wales coast. After the takeover the Menzies chairman could say (Vol. I, Number 1 of the Menzies-Wyman house magazine, December 1959) that the company now stretched from Thurso in Caithness to Penzance in Cornwall.

The prophecy–'We have not heard the end of the House of Menzies'–was fulfilled rather sooner than most observers expected. In the space of a week, in February 1961, Menzies's bought up two important provincial businesses, Pickles of Leeds and Porter of Belfast.

Charles Henry Pickles had been one of the pioneers of wholesaling in Yorkshire. He had opened his first wholesale warehouse in Leeds in 1892.

Attractive publications have commemorated some of the notable milestones in Menzies's history. This is the book of the 125th anniversary (1958).

He branched out to York (1899), to Huddersfield (1901), to Hull and Doncaster (1903), to Wakefield (1907) and to Dewsbury and Scarborough (1914). While on course for a big future he had been tragically hit by the First World War, losing more than a quarter of his staff, all the young men having joined up together. The deaths included that of his own son, Herbert Gladstone Pickles, the managing director designate. The firm slowly recovered and opened one or two branches in the north-east of England, the last being at Newcastle-upon-Tyne in 1927.

Coincidentally, the Pickles headquarters in Leeds stood opposite a pickling factory, and the staff grew quite accustomed to girls coming in about the advertisement for jobs in the bottling plant. When Pickles changed its name to Menzies one of the first customers went away in disgust because they wouldn't give him an assisted passage to Australia: the only Menzies he knew was the then prime minister of that country.

Like an arranged marriage between children of feudal landowners, the Menzies-Pickles union created an estate of imposing area. The name of Menzies, not long since confined to Scotland, was seen in Northumberland, Cumberland and Yorkshire and as far south as Scunthorpe in Lincolnshire.

Charles Porter & Company of Belfast had begun in a small way with newspapers and stationery in 1900. There were people in Belfast who remembered Charles himself delivering orders in his pony and trap–a pony called Tim in honour of the hero of the popular children's paper, *Tiger Tim's Weekly*. Moving with the times, Mr Porter acquired one of the first Model T Fords and then a small fleet of them, by which time the pony was enjoying retirement as a family pet. When Menzies's stepped in the firm was the principal wholesale stationer and newsagent in Northern Ireland.

Purchase of those two concerns brought the total of Menzies employees

Horace Marshall's publishing and wholesale distribution business used to be controlled from premises in Fleet Street, where the *Daily Express* building now stands. The advertisement, a familiar sight on the buses and tube escalators of the metropolis fifty years ago, incorporated a silhouette of London's skyline as seen from the upper floors of the building.

close to five thousand. (It's now more than seven thousand five hundred and the annual wage bill is £26 millions.)

Among the Scottish establishments which fell and were picked up by John Menzies were two bookshops of old-world dignity, McCallum's of Glasgow and Douglas & Foulis of Edinburgh. (The 'Douglas' was that bookseller neighbour of John Menzies the first in 1833; Edmonston & Douglas.) In London the firm collected Webster & Co. of Piccadilly and Frank Smythson's of Bond Street.

Webster, a stationer since 1780, published the *Badminton Diary* and had held the royal warrant of Queen Alexandra. Smythson's was–and still is, because exceptionally it has kept its own name under Menzies's owner-ship–another of those quality metropolitan houses which discerning people patronise and which no one who knows his London can afford not to know about. Nominally a stationer's, it's famous for its upmarket miscellany, 'from a tiepin to a cakestand'.

Long ago, by some oversight in the paper-making process, Smythson's received a consignment of superfine blue writing paper instead of super-fine white, and that year it had to bring out its diaries and address-books in blue. The colour and the texture caught on. The firm had its *cachet*. Should you meet someone in London carrying a parcel made up in flimsy 'blue bank' wrapping paper, you know they've been shopping at Smythson's. (At the royal wedding of 1981 Smythson's offered elegant lines in com-memorative paperweights, leather desk sets and English enamel boxes.)

In 1962 Menzies's were in London for another bid. Horace Marshall & Son, publishers and wholesalers, had for many years occupied the site of the *Daily Express* building in Fleet Street. The original Marshall had opened his first shop in 1840 and then his first railway bookstall–at Fenchurch

A foothold in Mayfair. Such was the prestige of this chic establishment in London's smartest shopping district that after its acquisition by John Menzies it was allowed to retain its own name.

Street station, claimed as the first bookstall site of all. Within ten years he had nearly all the bookstalls on the routes which were eventually incorporated in the G.W.R. system. He might have been a serious competitor for W.H. Smith, but his son and grandson saw no future in bookstalls.

The grandson became Lord Mayor of London and a peer. His son-in-law was J. Arthur Rank, afterwards Lord Rank, who succeeded him as chairman. On Lord Rank's retirement John Menzies acquired the business for £1 million. The practical effect was to increase Menzies's share of the wholesale trade in England.

After joining the Menzies group Horace Marshall & Son were combined with Wyman's and in 1964 the joint firm, known as Wyman Marshall Ltd, came under the administration of the parent company at Menzies House in Whitefriars Street, EC4. (Menzies House, the nerve-centre of the London and Home Counties operations, symbolised a presence which was to exert an increasing influence on the commercial life of the capital. The first Menzies House went up in Glasgow in 1957. It was a purpose-built warehouse seven stories high, with a façade of Aberdeen granite and Portland stone. It's the architectural pride of West Nile Street.)

When Wyman and Marshall were combined, two of Marshall's provincial subsidiaries lost their identity. They were Ernest Joyce & Company Ltd, originally of Cardiff and Newport (Gwent) with branches in Derby and East Anglia; and Roberts & Wrate Ltd, a household name in Hampshire and the Isle of Wight; both wholesale news distributors.

All those businesses were honoured in the trade for their antiquity. They bore the names of men who had been near-contemporaries of John Menzies the founder. Like him, they'd been clever, industrious, far-sighted entrepreneurs, seeing the potential of railways when railways were a novelty, appreciating the future of newspapers when newspapers were a costly luxury for the educated few.

Senior of them all was the house of Wyman. It had been founded in 1677 by a man who saw King Charles I go to the scaffold; though its history had something in common with the Irishman's antique knife, with its two new handles and three new blades. Always in the printing and publishing business, the firm had gone through the trading names of Tonson; Tonson & Watts; Watts; Watts & Cox; Cox & Son; Cox & Baylis; Cox & Henry; Cox Bros & Wyman; and, in 1872, Wyman & Sons. Under the last name it had opened its first railway bookstall in 1906 and, in a matter of weeks, had snatched the leases of three hundred and forty-nine more.

At the time of the Menzies bid the old name of Cox & Wyman was revived for the printing offshoot of the firm. This side was sold off after the takeover. Cox & Wyman have no connection with John Menzies today.

In the old basement, long and low and narrow, under Number 95 Bishopsgate in the City of London, twelve employees of Wyman Marshall used to gather nightly to make up, with a speed and dexterity incredible to behold if you hadn't seen it before, the national dailies and provincial and foreign newspapers for distribution round the financial square mile. The remarkable feature was the enormous number of tiny packages, for the area served was mostly offices, many of which subscribed only for the *Financial Times* or *The Times*.

These operations are now carried out by John Menzies's retail news delivery subsidiary, Jones Yarrell–a recent acquisition but a firm of venerable prestige, long associated with picturesque activities. They are the traditional suppliers of newspapers and periodicals to Buckingham Palace, Windsor Castle, the royal yachts and the Queen's flights.

The day dawned in 1960 when British Rail began energetically (some said ruthlessly) to implement the Beeching plan for streamlining the rail services and closing many stations–and the bookstalls with them. At the end of 1962 John Menzies bookstalls were at their numerical peak: three hundred and fifty-seven. (The figure had shot up when the firm acquired Wyman's.) Twelve months later they were down to three hundred and fifty. The slide continued steadily. Twenty years later the figure was more or less stable around sixty-seven.

For both financial and sentimental reasons the company lamented the closure of Edinburgh's Caledonian station, the nearest one to Menzies's headquarters. But on the whole it could well afford to lose the rest. The bookstalls had faced, as newsagents everywhere were facing, another problem of the affluent society: the difficulty in finding schoolchildren willing to get up early to serve in shops and make deliveries for a few shillings a week. Dwindling passenger traffic on the railways was naturally the big factor; more cars, more buses meant fewer people reading a newspaper on the way to work.

Old-fashioned people in country districts have told how they were left confused and lost by the closure of, for example, the Blair Atholl bookstall on the Perth-Inverness line. Such places had been for them a part of the unchanging landscape. But Blair Atholl, and scores of places like it, were by now, in the chairman's words, 'all small and relatively unprofitable'.

Another sign that an era was drawing to a close was the disappearance in 1966 of *Murray's Diary,* that ancient stand-by of the travelling public. It hadn't altered in price (one penny) for a hundred and twenty-four years.

Enlargement and elaboration of the metropolitan and city bookstalls accompanied the trimming of the rural stances. At any large rail terminus the term 'bookstall' was quite inadequate to describe the Menzies presence. They dealt in a vast range of merchandise and their turnovers were extraordinary by earlier standards. The size the station bookstall had grown to was revealed in a news item about the staff at Euston Colonnade. It numbered forty-two and comprised eighteen nationalities, including the Scottish manager and assistants from as far away as Thailand, Sri Lanka and Algeria.

Books still came first at the bookstall. That same Menzies stance at Euston station sold five thousand copies of Alistair Maclean's *Where Eagles Dare* in eight weeks; in a year (1969) notorious for publishers' complaints that no one bought books any more.

And still the City had 'not heard the last of John Menzies'. Significant organisational developments kept the name in the news. In 1960 the group of companies controlled by John Menzies & Company became John Menzies (Holdings) Ltd. Under Common Market regulations the 'Ltd' has since become 'plc'–public limited company.

In October 1962 it went public, announcing that its own employees at sixty-three depots, three hundred and thirty bookstalls and a hundred and seventeen shops would be invited to participate in the share issue. But the strong personal hold on a company which had always prided itself on being a family business was to be maintained. Of two and a half million ordinary shares issued, the Menzies family retained nearly two million. (In 1981 there was a new share-participation scheme. Employees with more than five years' service–a total of about eighteen hundred–became eligible for allocations of shares which were to be bought by trustees with a percentage of the annual pre-tax profits of the firm.)

Certain traditions which the post-war takeovers had brought along with them had to submit to the practical realities of commerce. The tidying-up of the trading names of the various subsidiaries was undertaken in 1967. Familiar titles like Wyman and Marshall had to go. Other titles, not so well known nationally although they meant a lot in their particular localities, were seen no more. The blue-and-white Menzies panels (first seen on the nameboard of Elliot's in Princes Street, Edinburgh, enlivened in November 1976 with an orange stripe, first seen at Menzies's in Stirling) decorated the façades of all the group's retail shops and stalls.

During 1969 a major administrative re-structuring took place. John Menzies (Holdings) Ltd, in which nine subsidiaries had submerged their identities, was split up into six divisions, each having a director of the company in charge: Wholesale, Retail, Commercial, Financial, Personnel and Property.

The company's future objective was expressed clearly and concisely: 'To concentrate resources on the activities which provide the optimum results'. That was to say, prune or sell off unprofitable outlets, buy up and expand profitable ones.

The name of WYMANS on delivery vans and bookstalls, widespread in the west of England, faded out in 1967 when the John Menzies sign replaced the trading names of the various subsidiaries.

11

'A business greatly extended'

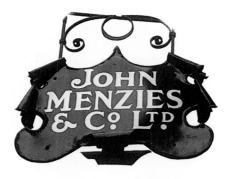

'A business greatly extended'

The large Menzies shop at
107 Princes Street, Edinburgh,
sited within a few yards of the little
bookshop at No. 61, which the
founder opened 150 years ago.

"Mr Menzies himself attended at the front counter and supplied demands from the Trade . . . his business in time greatly extended."

So said old James Thin the Edinburgh bookseller, reminiscing about events of the 1830s. If he could have looked forward to the 1980s, what would he make of the business now? How would he measure the broad torrents of merchandise, the lakes of newsprint and forests of newspaper which pour daily through Britain's letter-boxes? How could he comprehend the ramifications of services, the books, records, tapes, confectionery, stationery, toys, games and other accessories of leisure; and the high technology of communications with which the name of Menzies is associated today?

A couple of generations ago that 'unpronounceable' name was a sign to strangers that they had arrived in Scotland–by rail. Outside railway stations it wasn't seen. One generation ago you might come across it on bookstalls in England too, but still confined to railway stations. It seems like yesterday–in the context of company history it *was* yesterday–when the blue and white of a Menzies signboard first caught the eye in the shopping precincts of cities and towns all over Great Britain.

The Menzies shop is now a feature of many population centres. Many of them are quite new; all of them look new. They give that 'much-needed touch of brightness' that was approved by a Glasgow journalist long ago at St Enoch's station, they mediate between the drabness and garishness which characterise too much of the British urban scene. The staff ('the smartest . . . the slickest') clearly belong to a *corps d'élite*. John Menzies obviously takes seriously the promise which the founder made to the railway companies back in 1862; that his employees 'shall be in apparent good health, clean in their persons and apparel, and civil to customers'.

Like many another successful Scottish organisation, the house of Menzies can pride itself on steady progress over a long period rather than spectacular leaps. Considering the pitfalls of the years, it is remarkable that the forward movement should have been so consistent over three half-centuries of its history. It looks as though such progress was part of the natural order of things; but Mr J.C.M. Eason the Dublin wholesaler had something to say on that topic when he spoke at a booksellers' banquet and looked back at what people called the good old days:

"We must refrain from the common error of supposing that life ran smoothly then. We shall recognise fully that the past had its own difficulties; that alternative courses were always open to those in charge; that choice was not any easier then than it is now; that there was nothing inevitable about our history . . ."

What makes it more remarkable in the Menzies case is that a John Menzies has been at the helm, or very close to the helm, from the very start to the present day; a John Menzies in direct descent from the founder. Sons do not always take kindly to the dynastic role, nor are the parents' talents necessarily those of their children. Yet four generations have carried the Menzies torch for a hundred and fifty years. Two sons, moreover, were introduced to high office when very young. Our history shows that they were not overwhelmed by it.

The Training Centre in Regent Terrace, Edinburgh, where short residential courses are held for Menzies's managerial and area staff.

Menzies history over the past fifteen years has been a tale not only of expansion and consolidation but also of diversification down various paths. In 1969 the firm launched a training scheme for managers and area staff and opened a centre in Regent Terrace, Edinburgh. Residential courses of from one to five days are offered. From 1981 senior managers have been undergoing courses on subjects such as leadership, motivation and how to chair a meeting. Those with a sense of history might reflect how far the company has travelled since the first John Menzies suggested proficiency in needlework as the qualification for a person in charge of the bookstall at Bridge of Allan station.

Local radio reached eastern Scotland in 1974 and the firm took a stake in Radio Forth. Speaking on a current affairs programme, John M. Menzies said he hoped to see the shops catering for the family's leisure needs as well as its basic requirements. That had reference to the sportswear and sporting equipment which the larger shops had begun to sell and to the more volatile areas of here-today-and-gone-tomorrow pastimes, from skateboards to Rubik cubes, which they would soon be concerned with. Temporary crazes mean headaches for wholesalers: they cannot be ignored, but these days you don't keep stock on the shelves 'for twenty-five years and no sale' as the founder did with *The True Python's Oracle*.

New avenues have opened from activities within the firm. In the main Edinburgh shop there is now a travel agency. The Menzies team which did the interior design for the company's administrative offices in 1974 formed itself into a furniture-and-office-design subsidiary (D.P. Office Concepts Ltd, trading as Design Plus) and quickly won large contracts with Ind Coope the Midlands brewers and Sony the electronics firm. In 1981-2, a difficult year for office furnishers, Design Plus returned its first profit.

As a result of its own nationwide communications needs in 1974 John Menzies, in association with a Californian electronics firm called Wavetek, pioneered 'voice response', one of the earlier marvels of microchip technology. This was Menzies' first American connection. Within four years the company had its own voice-response marketing subsidiary, Menzies Communications Systems, and was supplying equipment to industry, notably the major motor manufacturers. M.C.S., operating in Britain and Germany, had a successful run over the first few years and in 1982 a tie-up with the Comdial corporation of San Francisco, leading developers of sophisticated telecommunications, was arranged.

The American connection was further strengthened in 1980, when Frank Smythson of Bond Street acquired the New York company which formerly distributed its diaries in the United States.

Books, on which the Menzies organisation was built, are not neglected. A notable subsidiary in that field is Children's Books (Rugeley) who distribute picture books, jigsaw puzzles and associated juvenilia from a delightful little factory in rural Staffordshire. Not far away, at Newcastle-under-Lyme, the well-known record distribution company of Terry Blood Ltd came under the John Menzies banner at a time when record sales nationwide were falling off. Terry Blood (Records) rode the recession well and are currently the biggest independent wholesalers of records, tapes and accessories in the United Kingdom.

In May 1982 John Menzies won the battle for Lonsdale Universal with a £6.3 million takeover bid. Lonsdale are a Middlesex company dealing with international library supply, commercial stationery and technical publications. (Incidentally Menzies are now the largest library suppliers in Australia.)

Menzies's have gone foreign in other ways. For some years the Belfast warehouse (which has had its share of troubles, as may be imagined) has supplied retail shops in the Republic of Ireland. A rather picturesque link with Iceland is no more: consignments of books, magazines and newspapers from Menzies' Warrington branch used to be sent down to Runcorn docks once a fortnight for passage to Reykjavik in the motor vessel *Kjalfoss*, a service now suspended.

For two decades the railway bookstalls, which at one period kept the Menzies name before the public, have been declining numerically. It is still true to say, as the *Northern Chronicle* said long ago of Aberdeen, that 'the business done is enormous'. But many of the smaller outlets have had to go, have been converted to other uses and have lost that 'very pretty kiosque-like appearance', which the *Inverness Courier* once admired. New constructions and acquisitions do not quite replace over-age or unprofitable discards and the total is now around seventy. A good example of a modern Menzies bookstall is at the Birmingham International railway station, built in 1976 and serving the airport and the National Exhibition Centre.

Branches have overtaken bookstalls. There are now eighty-seven of these regional offices and warehouses and wholesale distribution centres. The total is not expected to alter significantly although, where space permits, some branches may expand.

The growth area over the past quarter-century has been the retail shops. For the first hundred years of its history, the firm managed with one. Then, in the 1930s, it opened two more. Nowadays the figure is around the two-hundred mark, plus or minus occasional new acquisitions and occasional disposals.

The largest shops in England are at Maidstone, Shrewsbury and Bournemouth, not that they are the biggest towns but because the cubic capacity of the premises happened to be the most generous. In the north, Edinburgh, Glasgow and Dundee have the largest shops. The main Glasgow shop, in all-pedestrian Buchanan Street, paid £100,000 in rates for 1981-2, without having taken up its full capacity. It will never do so, for the company has decided to move this shop to new premises in Glasgow's Argyle Street.

Buchanan Street, however, has its niche in Menzies history. Advance publicity for the opening in 1974 whipped up a lot of interest and the staff speculated on a stampede. But they were unprepared for the multitudes who massed round the main doors a full forty-eight hours before the inauguration. All was explained when the manager fought his way through to find a rock-singer giving an impromptu recital, with his guitar plugged into a Menzies switchbox which hadn't been sealed down.

In Edinburgh's Princes Street there are now two Menzies shops overlooking the Castle rock, the gardens and the roofs of the diesel trains which run back and forth in the cutting parallel with the street–the cutting which John Menzies the founder saw being excavated. And the colour schemes of the trains, blue and yellow, appropriately enough reflect the colours of an organisation which built itself up with the railways.

The biggest shop of all, Number 107 Princes Street, employs more than a hundred assistants. (At Number 61, in the next block, the founder employed one.) The upper floors of this building contain the administrative offices of John Menzies. Over the years the firm's headquarters have moved about, hollowing out more room but never straying more than a few hundred yards from its birthplace. Of all the merchants of ambition and high hopes who took over the first properties in Scotland's most famous thoroughfare, none but John Menzies remains there.

Behind Princes Street in the middle 1970s the main warehouse, Hanover Buildings, underwent a transformation. The old-fashioned office equipment, magazine shelves and counters yielded to video displays, computer print-outs and tables of processed data incomprehensible to the uninitiated . . . signs of the times, slightly ahead of which it has always been the Menzies ambition to move.

In the course of our history we have noted changes of title: from John Menzies in 1833 to John Menzies & Company in 1867; to John Menzies & Company Ltd in 1906; to John Menzies (Holdings) Ltd in 1960. In March 1982 the name was altered again to John Menzies plc–public limited company. It has since been decided that in future the company will be known as John Menzies plc.

The company's turnovers and profits have increased with seemingly uncanny regularity year by year through boom and recession, industrial peace and industrial turmoil, through all the uncertainties of the markets and periods of rise and fall in what economists call 'consumer disposable income'–in other words, how much we can afford to spend.

In 1833 John Menzies reported his profits as 'very small'. By the time he died (1879) they had moved up to about £5,000 a year. At the date of the company's incorporation, 1906, they jumped from £8,000 to £15,000. In the 1930s, aided by inflation, they were around £100,000 a year. Twelve months after the company went public the pre-tax profits topped the £½ million mark.

Nine years on Menzies's had attained pre-tax profits of nearly £1 million. For the year ending January 1981 they were £7.6 millions. 'John Menzies has again demonstrated that a well-run company can overcome recessions, industrial dislocations and high interest rates . . . one clue to Menzies's success is that the group regards obstacles to the continued expansion of its business as challenges to be overcome'–the *Glasgow Herald* in the sort of tribute which had become typical in the financial pages of the press when the company reported its annual position.

Pre-tax profits in the year ending January 1982 were £9.4 millions. The British Institute of Management cited Menzies's as one of the 45 (out of the top 200) British companies, whose results had beaten inflation. It appears, as this history is concluded that the chairman's hopes of matching the magic figure of 150 years of age in February 1983 with the magic figure of £10 millions pre-tax profits may well be realised.

The balance sheet does not mean much to the ordinary customer but it helps to determine whether a commercial concern is to maintain or improve or cut back its service to the public. It has a bearing on those prompt deliveries; and on that warm, well-lit, well-stocked, well-staffed store.

Tradition has a bearing too. Indeed, tradition is the vital ingredient, providing the underlying strength of the past and the incentive for the future. 'Large, handsome and varied supplies' . . . 'a constant and enticing choice' . . . 'a boon much appreciated by the public'–when you have been in business for 150 years you cannot help hearing echoes of the compliments you have collected along the way. A few have been quoted in this book, the object of which has been to show the times the house of Menzies has lived through; and the reputation it has to live up to.

Head office of John Menzies plc, Princes Street, Edinburgh. The firm's headquarters has always been based within the same inner-city square mile of Edinburgh's capital.

The Menzies Dynasty

Some Menzies Directors

The Menzies Dynasty

John Menzies was born in Edinburgh in 1808, attended the Royal High School and was apprenticed to a bookseller. He worked briefly in London and in 1833 opened the first Menzies shop at 61 Princes Street, Edinburgh, where he sold and published books and engravings. In 1857 he began acquiring bookstalls on railway stations and at the same time building up a wholesale newspaper distributing organisation. He established John Menzies & Company in 1867 and opened the firm's first branch in Glasgow. He died in 1879.

John Ross Menzies ('John R.') was born in 1852 and became head of the firm when his father died. He was Menzies's first chairman when it became a limited company in 1906. He retired in 1927, resigned as chairman in 1932 and died unmarried in 1935.

Charles Thompson Menzies ('Colonel Charles'), born 1858, became assistant head of the firm at the age of twenty-two. He married Helen Aitken, daughter of the leading Falkirk brewer. He was M.F.H. of the Berwickshire Hunt, an appointment he handed over to his wife when, as an officer in the county yeomanry, he went to Flanders on war service in 1916. He followed his brother as chairman of Menzies's in 1932. Death terminated the appointment in 1943, after which his widow held the chairmanship until 1951. With sixty-four years' service, Charles Thompson is the firm's longest-serving 'employee'.

John Francis Marr Menzies was born in 1900. After Eton he trained with W.H. Smith & Son and entered the family business in 1921. He died suddenly in 1940, at which time he was vice-chairman of the company. He married Cynthia Graham. His sister Helen (Margaret) married Admiral Sir Bertram Ramsay.

Charles Cuthbert Menzies, born 1905, followed his brother to Eton, went on to Cambridge, joined the firm in 1926 and was a director when he went into the Royal Air Force in 1941. On his return in 1945 he was appointed vice-chairman. Six years later he too died suddenly.

John Maxwell Menzies, born in 1926, is the great grandson of the founder. After Eton and service with the Grenadier Guards he joined the firm in 1948 and in 1951 became chairman, a position he has held ever since. In 1953 he married the daughter of Commander Sir Hugh Dawson, Bart. He holds directorships in several outside companies.

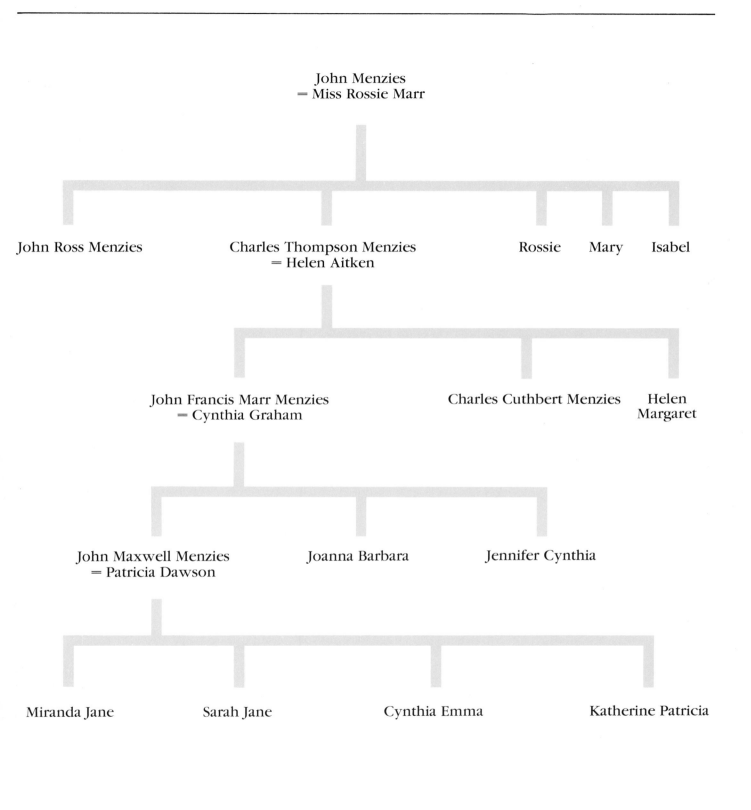

John Menzies
= Miss Rossie Marr

John Ross Menzies   Charles Thompson Menzies   Rossie   Mary   Isabel
                           = Helen Aitken

John Francis Marr Menzies   Charles Cuthbert Menzies   Helen
= Cynthia Graham   Margaret

John Maxwell Menzies   Joanna Barbara   Jennifer Cynthia
= Patricia Dawson

Miranda Jane   Sarah Jane   Cynthia Emma   Katherine Patricia

Some Menzies Directors

Peter Nisbet (director 1910-1940): when the house of Menzies was incorporated in 1906 he became the first company secretary. In his younger days he had been an assistant to John R. and Charles T. Menzies and generally acknowledged their right-hand man and confidant. Between 1915 and 1931, as general manager, he piloted the company through some of its most difficult years. He died in harness in 1940, aged seventy-five.

James Robertson (director 1917-1945): another accountant, who took over the company secretaryship from Peter Nisbet in 1911. He was also the chief bookstall inspector. He followed Peter Nisbet again in 1931, this time into the general manager's chair, and when Charles T. Menzies died in 1943 he became managing director. He retired at seventy, in 1945, and died nine years later.

James Anderson (director 1931-1956): a soldier and a chartered accountant who joined the firm in 1919 at the age of thirty. Within a few years he was company secretary and then a director. He took over the managing directorship in 1946 and held the post for eight critical years. He died in 1961, aged seventy-two.

Herbert Maxwell Graham (director 1932-1965): joined Menzies's in 1926, after youthful service in the Royal Navy, and was appointed to the board at the age of twenty-seven. On return from service in World War II he became a vice-chairman and afterwards (1959) vice-chairman of John Menzies (Holdings) Ltd. Author of a short history of the Menzies group, to which the present author has been indebted. "A great help to me when I was younger," says the present chairman. Mr Graham retired in 1965 and died in 1982.

Reginald Nussey (director 1945-1970): a good example of a bright boy marked out and groomed for advancement. Starting as a clerk at the Carlisle branch, he was chief branch inspector at thirty and a director at thirty-nine, in which capacity he helped guide the company's fortunes through World War II. He was managing director after James Anderson and, on the formation of John Menzies (Holdings) Ltd in 1959, became its first managing director. He retired in 1970.

Thomas P. Callaghan (director 1962-   ): another young man who climbed to the top through the ranks. He joined the firm in 1937, aged fourteen, and after war service proceeded via branch inspectorships to the boardroom. A managing director of John Menzies & Co Ltd from 1962, he was appointed wholesale managing director of John Menzies (Holdings) Ltd in 1979.

David F. Ramsay (director 1960-   ): a great-grandson of the founder, he joined the firm in 1957 after leaving Cambridge. He became an executive director in 1960 and a non-executive director in 1973, when his principal activity became investment research.

Douglas G. MacDonald (director 1968-   ): a graduate of St Andrews University and a former Cameron Highlander, he was appointed managing director of the Menzies subsidiary Wyman Marshall in 1966 and became managing director of the Menzies group in 1971. He holds several outside directorships, and in 1982 was appointed chairman of the Scottish Council's Research Institute.